What Others are
Life on Pause

Waiting is hard! Waiting beats down our faith and strength. Everyone waits for something. As we know, everyone experiences taxes and death, but we can add a third surety: waiting. Have no fear about your coming season of waiting or your present unmet desire. Candy Arrington's book *Life on Pause* will prepare you with faith, confidence, and trust in God who, though the creator of waiting, is waiting to strengthen you to trust Him no matter how eager you are to end the waiting period. I highly value the wisdom and encouragement Candy offers, with a delightful mixture of personal stories and Bible inspiration. Read this book! Your faith will grow.

~Kathy Collard Miller, international speaker and author of more than 55 books including *God's Intriguing Questions: 60 New Testament Devotions Revealing Jesus's Nature*

Waiting is a holy time, as much of a gift from God as the times of joy and love. Candy Arrington offers ways for us to treasure the waiting time, and to accept and to submit to it, trusting in the Father, whose plans for us are always good. Candy's stories, and those of others, show that while we all live in a "right now" world, waiting and trusting are blessings. There's no preaching in this book. Candy's encouraging tone and vulnerability provide food for the reader's journey.

~Melanie Rigney, author, *Woman of Worth: Prayers and Reflections for Women Inspired by the Book of Proverbs* (Twenty-third Publications)

Hurry up and wait has been my mantra pretty much my whole life. But it was in the seasons of being forced to pause that God showed up the brightest and the best. We pray for patience, forgetting how patience comes about. And yet, those times of being honed for patience are the times when God gives us the grace we need in such abundance we almost cannot drink it in fast enough. Candy Arrington's message of waiting ... not necessarily on God, but with God, is timely and much needed in our world today.

~Eva Marie Everson, Bestselling & Award-winning Author & Speaker, President, Word Weavers International, Inc.

Life on Pause could easily be titled On Waiting Well as Candy provides for impatient people what William Zinsser's *On Writing Well* does for the writing industry. *Life on Pause* is a handbook for the hurried and a balm for the frustrated. Tired of waiting for change to happen, cars to get out of your way, promises to be fulfilled ... a pandemic to end? Candy's candid examples and biblical guidance helped me change my negative perspective on waiting to an attitude of peace. Now I feel more equipped to be a positive influence in these situations.

~Beth Patch, Senior Editor/Producer for CBN.com

Life on Pause uncovers treasures found in the power of trusting God. Candy Arrington will help you see there is no need to worry about timing as you unwrap God's gifts hidden in every delay. Learn how to turn unexpected interruptions into a rendezvous with God's transforming power.

~Linda Evans Shepherd, author of *Praying Through Every Emotion*, is the founder of the Advanced Writers & Speakers Association and the Arise Esther Movement.

Life on Pause is the book we've been waiting for. We all face delays and detours, and author Candy Arrington digs deep into her faith and knowledge of God's word to share applicable truths to help us cope. Truly a book I'll return to again and again.

~Edie Melson, award-winning author and Director of the Blue Ridge Mountains Christian Writers Conference

Through her own poignant stories, and those of others, author Candy Arrington clearly demonstrates she knows how to wait, and she's learned to do it well. You will find *Life on Pause* to be a truly encouraging book. It contains practical steps and scripture to guide you as you walk through your own season of waiting. If you're not in a period of waiting today, you can be certain you soon will be! This book will equip you to wait with faith and perseverance.

~Sharon Tedford, author, speaker, singer, songwriter, podcaster, and director of "61 Things" ministry.

Waiting isn't one of my virtues, and I suspect it isn't for many people. But as Candy Arrington shares in her wonderful new book, *Life on Pause,* there are valuable lessons to be learned during waiting seasons. God always has a purpose for those times in our lives, and Candy's wisdom, based on God's Word, will bless, comfort, and inspire you as you wait.

~Michelle Cox, award-winning, best-selling author of the *When God Calls the Heart series* and *Just 18 Summers*

Waiting is hard for everyone. Yet there are times when we have to wait. Candy Arrington helps readers understand and thrive in these challenging situations.

W. Terry Whalin, Bestselling author and editor
www.terrywhalin.com

I once heard a comedian joke about how long it takes to wait for something to update on a smart phone. "Don't you realize," he exclaimed, "that your request just went into outer space, bounced off a satellite, travelled somewhere in the world, bounced back off the satellite, then returned to your phone? What are you complaining about?"

Have you ever imagined the intricate details that need to fall into place in order for God's will to be worked out in your life? It's mind-blowing to think of all the events that have to take place and all the decisions that have to be made by people we don't even know in order for our prayers to be answered in a certain situation.

So, like this comedian said, "What are we complaining about?" And yet it can be so difficult to wait for God's plan to unfold in our lives.

In her book, *Life on Pause*, author Candy Arrington gives biblical and practical advice for remaining patient while God does the miracle of bringing His will to pass in your life. By following these timeless principles, your faith will grow as you watch God move heaven and earth to fulfill His plan, in His time!

- Dr. Craig von Buseck, Author and Managing Editor of Inspiration.org

Waiting is rarely easy, yet our lives are filled with situations where we must wait. Fortunately, Candy Arrington has given us a plan. *Life on Pause* provides us with suggestions of what to do while we are waiting and how to look to God for strength during those difficult times. Candy and her husband Jim have found themselves in the waiting room many times during their lives and every time God has provided answers to all their questions. What you'll find in this book is largely from personal experience and for those who know Candy Arrington, they know she lives what she writes.

Linda Gilden, Author, speaker, editor, writing coach, Cofounder of the LINKED® Personality System, Director of the Carolina Christian Writers Conference

Life on Pause

Life on Pause

Learning to Wait Well

Candy Arrington

Bold Vision Books
PO Box 2011
Friendswood, Texas 77549

Information on Scripture versions located on page 182

Dedication

To Jim

I'm thankful for this journey we share.
In the joys, sorrows, and even in the
waiting, we us.

Ecclesiastes 4:12 GNT

Table of Contents

Foreword

Waiting is the constant companion of every human being. We all do it and all the time. Even babies let you know they are waiting to be fed. The very thought of waiting can produce the entire spectrum of human emotions, from keen anticipation and expectation, to serious anxiety and concern.

Recently my wife and I waited for word from our daughter. She serves the Lord in Africa with a great Christian organization and departed the United States after a short visit home. Every step of the journey seemed to present a fresh set of obstacles. "I have landed safely," sounded more like the "Hallelujah Chorus" than a mere statement of fact.

A bereaved family recently shared with me that the death of their loved one provided much needed relief when compared to the long days and lonely nights as they waited for suffering to end and God's angels to arrive.

For almost three decades, I have had the joy of knowing Candy Arrington and her family. She is a most loving wife, mother, grandmother, friend, and very faithful Christian lady of the highest order. Candy lives out what she writes.

This wonderful book rings the bell loud and clear. *Life on Pause* is so well-written. Easy to read, it flows with the practical reality of this human predicament we are all certain to have. We cannot escape the fact we all start at birth and then grow up every day of our lives. Each step along the way introduces fresh opportunities to wait. It is as if we are all perpetually hanging on the edge of our next season of waiting.

This book really helps to give the reader a concrete hope during the long days of the wait. It is on target in terms of its biblical base, and it flows with the practical reality of our daily lives. Candy's use of real-life illustrations really helps to drive the point home. And how could this subject be more relevant than in today's world? Although Candy may not have had COVID-19 in mind when she first developed the idea, God evidently did. In a world of hypertension, restlessness, and significant discouragement, the author's words are so needed today.

I love this book because it helps me negotiate my daily struggles and challenges as I wait for my next. It shows me where to go and offers me both inner and outer places to go, even with my vast array of emotions. Most of us struggle with our wait, and many of us are not even sure what we are waiting for. I heartily recommend this book for you and as a gift to a friend. As you experience *Life on Pause*, you can wait on the Lord. He will renew your strength.

~Dr. Don Wilton, Pastor, First Baptist Spartanburg, The Encouraging Word Broadcast Ministry, Pastor to Dr. Billy Graham

Acknowledgments

With overwhelming gratitude:

- To Jim for encouragement, support, eagle-eye editing, and navigating life pauses with me.

- To Penny, Kathy, Jeslyn, Jay, Mae Frances, Cindy, Jack, and Marva for sharing your waiting stories.

- To Karen and George Porter for understanding my vision for this book and offering a contract.

- To friends and family who prayed for me while I wrote and juggled other big, hard projects and challenges.

- To my pastor, Dr. Don Wilton, for providing spiritual wisdom and focus during a pandemic, and for writing a foreword.

- To the One who inspires, guides, and gives me words, Soli Deo Gloria.

Introduction

When I wrote the proposal for this book, signed the contract, and began writing, the word "coronavirus" and the acronym "COVID" were not part of my vocabulary. But early in 2020, these words burst into our world and changed our lives. Social distancing, job losses, closed stores and restaurants, daily national and local health crisis briefings, and masks became our new normal. We transitioned to work-from-home offices and virtual conferences, meetings, and learning.

Along with these changes, we were plunged into a season of waiting—waiting to see how long we would need to self-quarantine, waiting to see which businesses would weather closings without folding, waiting for restocking of supplies, waiting to see who would become infected with the virus, and waiting to see who would survive and who would not.

Life pauses are never welcome. We are a people of action and willfulness and being forced to wait goes against our natures. Yet, during times of waiting, we slow down, to ponder, to assess and reassess, to accept, and when waiting is over, to move forward.

Most of us view waiting negatively, but if we are receptive and perceptive, waiting teaches, enlightens, protects, and prepares for what lies ahead.

As is often the case, I was addressing my impatience with waiting and writing to readers when I wrote this book. May it encourage and minister to you in your time of waiting.

Chapter 1

Waiting When It's Hard

*Don't be impatient. Wait for the Lord, and he will
come and save you! Be brave, stouthearted, and
courageous. Yes, wait and he will help you.*

Psalm 27:14 TLB

In this age of high-speed Internet, search engines, and cell phones, we have instant access to information at our fingertips, or by asking a voice-activated assistant like Alexa or Siri. If we want to know the distance between where we are and where we're going, we type a location into a map app, and the distance and time required to travel appear. We can even gain information about delays along various routes to allow the opportunity for re-routing a trip prior to leaving, or to make adjustments along the way.

If curiosity prompts a search for information about a person, place, or event, we can find a list of sources after typing a few words. With fingers, or voice, we can connect immediately to a desired service or person, request items or information, make appointments, or order products almost instantaneously. Television advertising and infomercials often prompt rapid action with the words "don't wait" or "don't miss out" with the implication that waiting results in dire consequences.

Because we are so conditioned to immediacy, waiting has a negative connotation. From traffic snarls to drive-thru lines to prolonged periods of what feels like nothing is happening, we chafe at delays. Most of us overload our schedules, don't allow enough travel time, and are usually running a little late. Then we hit a construction zone or traffic accident and are suddenly forced to wait. Waiting is something most of us don't do well. We find waiting difficult because it requires patience, a commodity in short supply in today's hurry-up world.

Waiting Comes When You Least Expect It

Several years ago, my husband and I entered a waiting season.

Eleven months before that time of waiting began, my husband was called into a meeting on a Monday morning and told his job of over thirty years was terminated. We were in the middle of an extensive contractor-supervised home renovation project, and Jim had just purchased a new car following a rear-end collision that totaled his.

To say we were stunned by the loss of his job is an understatement. Not only was our income gone, but almost as an afterthought, as my husband left the severance meeting that morning, the human resources manager announced, "Oh, and your healthcare coverage terminates at midnight tonight." Those words were perhaps more devastating than the loss of income.

Within days, Jim sent job applications, and three weeks later, he started a new job. We breathed a sigh of relief, praised God for his provision, and went about our lives as normally as possible because our home was still a construction zone.

Looking back, that job loss was a test run for what was ahead, although we didn't know it. The first job loss felt like a hiccup. The next one was more significant.

When the project Jim was hired for was put on hold, and at the end of a workday, he found himself in another termination meeting. Thus, our season of waiting began.

At first, we weren't that concerned. After all, a year before he'd found a job within a few weeks, so we expected the same scenario. However, this time the market for his field had shifted and jobs were not as plentiful. As days stretched into weeks, and weeks rolled into months, we experienced the opportunity to test and strengthen our trust muscles.

We also practiced patience. "Practice" is an appropriate word to use with patience because cultivating patience involves a lot of trying and failing and practicing some more.

One day, as we approached the four-month mark, I read 1 Samuel 7. In this passage, the Israelites were in imminent danger. As the Philistines advanced and prepared to attack, the Israelites succumbed to fear. They petitioned Samuel to pray to the Lord on their behalf. The Lord answered Samuel's prayers by confusing the Philistine army with "God's thundering great voice." The Israelites advanced and won the battle. Afterwards, Samuel erected a stone in the place of victory, naming it Ebenezer (stone of help), and said, "Thus far, the Lord has helped us."

These words seemed to jump off the page as I read them. I wrote them on an index card and placed the card in the center of our kitchen table as a reminder that even though our season of waiting felt endless, God had not abandoned us "thus far."

Maybe you are in a season of waiting and need a "thus far" reminder. Waiting blinds us to the "thus fars" of God's provision and sustaining power. Spend some time thinking about Ebenezer moments in your waiting period. List them, and track evidence of God's provision in your journey.

The Impatience of Waiting

Until our grandchildren were born, I'd forgotten how quickly a baby becomes impatient when there is a delay in feeding time. At first, there are little grunting noises. Then, a little frown, a grimace, an open mouth, followed by a warm-up "waah." If food is still not forthcoming, the "waah" becomes a "waah-waah" and then a "waah-waah-waah," followed by a full-out yell. If the baby has cried long enough to get mad, even when the food source is placed close to his mouth, he takes a few seconds to slow his wails enough to realize the waiting is over.

Sometimes we are like babies when forced to wait. We want what we want immediately and become angry with even a short delay. Our perception of waiting and the biblical perspective are far different. What if, instead of thinking about what we can do to speed along, our minds went to God's purposes for the wait and what he is teaching us in the process?

Learning is something most of us want to skip. We'd like to have knowledge without having to go through the process of study and retention, but time is involved in learning, and for some, learning is a more involved process. Waiting may be solely designed to draw you closer to God and help you learn in ways only he can teach.

"If we want to live wider and deeper lives, not just faster ones, we have to practice patience— patience with ourselves, with other people, and with the big and small circumstances of life itself."

~M. J. Ryan
The Power of Patience

Patience

When news of a novel coronavirus, COVID-19, first appeared in headlines, most of us paid little attention, thinking it was something resulting from unsanitary conditions in an open-air market in a province in China. But as COVID-19 spread, and infected thousands of people in Europe, other parts of the world, and finally America, this virus became commonplace in conversation and changed our way of life.

To slow the spread of the virus and minimize the death toll, national and state mandates closed businesses and schools, shuttered churches, and canceled conferences. The fallout produced shortages, tanked the stock market, furloughed workers, and quarantined families in their homes. As we entered a season of watching and waiting, fears increased, even as many became irritable about restrictions that altered day-to-day life and created stress and financial strain.

After weeks of stay-at-home orders and closed businesses, people pushed back against restrictions, opening businesses ahead of time, and protesting with violent demonstrations. Besides fear, anger is an emotion that sometimes emerges during a life pause, overshadowing reason and perpetrating adverse actions and reactions.

Patience is an unwanted and unused word in the vocabulary of many. Patience involves self-discipline, the will to halt impulsiveness, and calmly accept a situation without complaining. Selfishness is the underlying factor in impatience. Selfishness demands personal rights above concern for others, and screams, "I want my way, now!"

Self-Control

Scripture teaches self-control, but many do not successfully master it. From food choices and purchases to self-expression, we are often out of control, barreling forward with obtaining what we want and think we need, despite the fallout to relationships, health, and finances.

Any form of self-control requires consistent effort in denying impulsive urges and acquisitions. Self-focus is at the heart of the lack of self-control, wanting what we want and obtaining it without delay.

Lack of verbal self-control is evident daily on social media in those who post excessive details about physical conditions and procedures to 300-word rants about some issue on which the person has strong opinions. Verbal self-control requires thinking before speaking or writing, allowing a waiting period to re-think words and cool emotions, and consideration for how your words will impact others.

Self-control is vital in times of waiting because it prevents rushing ahead with decisions or actions that may have negative consequences or impede God's plans for your future.

Humility

Humility is one of those illusive qualities that is hard to grasp. Just when you think you understand it, you realize you don't.

Humility requires effort. You can't tell others you're working toward it because it's a quality you cultivate silently, sharing your efforts only with God. If you already view yourself as humble, you're probably not.

Most people don't practice humility because it's a quality rarely modeled in those around us. Society says, "you deserve it!" The world teaches lifestyles of selfishness, pride, and greed. Often, those in leadership positions who fail do so because of an arrogant lack of humility. Arrogance doesn't respect the opinions of others and ignores facts, suggestions, and warnings.

A season of waiting may be specifically designed to help you cultivate the attribute of humility. While it may be a painful process to do the honest self-evaluation involved, humility is a quality that will move you forward when your waiting season ends.

Trust

Years ago, I attended a retreat that included team-building activities. We helped each other climb, balance, jump, and maneuver through obstacles. Near the end of the experience, we participated in a "trust fall." The "fallee" stands with her back to her team, crosses her arms in front and then falls backwards, trusting her teammates will catch her before she slams into the ground.

"Fallees" respond in various ways prior to falling. Some repeat "are you ready?" numerous times. Others look over their shoulders repeatedly to make sure teammates are poised and ready. And then, there are those who just cannot summon what is required to fall into the waiting arms of trust.

Waiting builds and strengthens trust muscles. Chapter 6 provides a more in-depth look at the role of trust in waiting.

The Consequences of Not Waiting

Many of us can remember times in our lives when we didn't consult God and allowed impatience to control our decisions. Penny's story underscores the negative results of failing to wait for God's timing.

Penny's Story

"We had outgrown our home and were excited about moving to a bigger house. The new house was close to the park where our boys' football teams practiced, saving me hours of driving. The "For Sale" sign went up at our house, but not much happened. A few people looked at it, but no offers. I was impatient because I wanted to move before the school year started.

"Waiting is hard for me. I'm not too fond of delays, especially since I had everything planned. The first day of school was approaching, and we still hadn't sold our house. Then, out of the blue, a buyer made an acceptable offer, and we packed. I felt we should move before we sold the old house and get a bridge loan until we had the money. My husband wasn't keen on the idea, but I persuaded him, and asked my parents to loan us the money for just a short term. They were not in favor of our decision either, but I convinced them everything would go well. After all, we had a buyer and would close in a few weeks. So, we forged ahead, borrowed the money, signed the papers, and moved.

"As we loaded the last few boxes into the new house, the buyer for our house backed out. Now we would have two mortgages and still owe my parents the money for the bridge loan. Several days after moving, we received a letter from the school district advising us of mandatory school busing. Our children would ride a bus for 45 minutes each way to an inner-city school. We decided to send them to a private school, which meant more money out of our already dwindling savings.

"Several weeks after moving into our new house, we noticed large cracks in the concrete in the driveway, garage, and basement floors. Then the ceiling in the middle of our house split apart. We learned the builder had not used the proper footings when building the house. I was extremely sorry I had pushed to move.

"For the next six months, we could not landscape or use the garage or basement. Each side of the house went on hydraulic jacks as workers put it back into place. They poured new concrete for the entire basement, garage, driveway, sidewalks, and front porch. Could anything else possibly go wrong?

"When the major part of the re-construction began, we drove to California for the children's fall break. We returned to a house reeking of spoiled food. The main power line to the house had been cut by the workers, most likely on the first day of our vacation. Everything in the freezer and refrigerator was rancid. Why did I push to move?

"Finally, we realized the error of taking matters into our hands, failing to consult God about our plans, and moving forward instead of waiting for God's timing. We had the perfect opportunity to stay where we were, because the contract for the new house was contingent on the sale of our home.

"After many months of double house payments, tuition at the private school, and the colossal headaches of extensive repairs to the house, we understood our monstrous mistake. Red flags were flying in our faces, but we ignored them. We learned costly lessons with that move, but thankfully God's grace allowed us to grow from our mistakes.

"Eventually, we sold the old house, sold the new house, paid my parents for the bridge loan, and moved back to our old neighborhood, where the kids were able to walk to school. Running ahead of God, instead of waiting for his best, was a huge lesson for us."

The Hard Truth of Waiting

Undergoing a physical examination is not something most of us look forward to, because the doctor usually points out some area in which we aren't doing as well as we could. Perhaps the need to lose a few pounds is part of the discussion or lab results show unhealthy eating habits.

A life pause may prove similar to a physical check-up. Although we might not like it, God allows waiting to discipline or refocus us.

Discipline

Spanking was an acceptable, and used, form of discipline when I was a child. I still remember the look on my mother's face when she announced, "I'm going to the switch tree!" I'd watch from the window as she marched across the yard and plucked a slim branch from the Nandina bush, stripping the leaves off as she walked back to the house. Once inside, the switch went on top of the refrigerator with a few inches protruding over the edge, a dangling reminder of discipline ahead if I didn't "straighten up and fly right."

"You have one more chance to obey me. If you don't, you'll get a switching."

The rewards of obedience and the consequences of disobedience are documented throughout Scripture. While God doesn't always use waiting to discipline, sometimes he does. More than likely, you know if a time of waiting is related to willful disobedience. If you are wise, you will accept the discipline and learn from it.

The Lord corrects the people he loves and disciplines those he calls his own. Be patient when you are being corrected!

Hebrews 12:6-7 CEV

Refocus

When you have an eye exam, part of the assessment requires looking into a machine at a bright white screen with a gray rectangle in the middle. The instructions are to look at the rectangle and click a handheld device every time you see squiggly lines appear on the screen. At first, the squiggly lines are obvious, and your clicks form a pattern. Then, there is a delay. You wait and feel a twinge of panic when you don't see more squiggles. Are you missing the obvious? Is something wrong with your vision? When you see squiggles again, you breathe a sigh of relief and click. Suddenly, the screen looks black. What's wrong? Panic returns. As if the technician senses your distress, she says, "blink if you need to."

Like an eye exam, waiting provides an opportunity to blink. The goals and plans you had in place before you entered a season of waiting may drift into your peripheral vision as new objectives take shape. Although you may experience a sense of panic at the shift, don't be afraid to blink and refocus. Resist the voice that says, "something is wrong," and allow a new vision to emerge.

For still the vision awaits its appointed time; it hastens to the end—it will not lie. If it seems slow, wait for it; it will surely come; it will not delay.

Habakkuk 2:3 ESV

The Journey of Waiting

When I was a child, our family took lots of driving vacations, the kind where you pack up the car with provisions for a week or ten days, and then hit the road with a loose itinerary. We'd drive for hours and stop for lunch near some attraction, walk through a battleground or museum, and then get back in the car for more driving.

Late in the afternoon, my parents would consult a map, one of those multi-fold kind that is as wide as the car, for towns farther down the road that might have a suitable place to spend the night. Sometimes, they'd stop at a pay phone to call ahead to check for vacancies (no cell phones or Internet in those days). Other times, instead of calling ahead, they would scope out motels as we drove by and stop if one seemed acceptable. That method often involved multiple stops if motels were full. After finding lodging, we'd eat supper, sleep, and then get up and do it all again.

As an only child, this type of journey, which felt like waiting all day for not much of a reward, was miserable. I wasn't far enough along in my life's journey to appreciate the difference in routine, the scenery, and the meaning behind historic sights.

A wise friend often says, "Remember to enjoy the journey." Since I am more of a destination-driven, make-a-list-and-check-it-off kind of person, the first time I heard this, it was a strange concept to me. Even now, years later, I zoom forward mentally to a time when a hard, challenging, or uncomfortable life season is over. If I can just finish this, make it through that, accomplish this goal, move beyond these emotions … everything will be better.

When life places us in a holding pattern, we have the option to accept the journey and learn from it or resist and complain. Yet, often, we are so intent on reaching what we consider to be the destination that we sprint through the journey without gleaning life lessons. We are all about attaining rather than learning through the process.

While you may think there is nothing enjoyable about waiting, you choose to discover positive aspects of the journey and benefit from them.

Consider it a sheer gift, friends, when tests and challenges come at you from all sides. You know that under pressure, your faith-life is forced into the open and shows its true colors. So don't get out of anything prematurely. Let it do its work so you become mature and well-developed, not deficient in any way.

James 1:2-4 THE MESSAGE

Roadblocks and Detours

Sometimes life feels like the road trips of childhood—a series of stops, delays, detours, re-routes, and roadblocks. You may have your course all mapped out only to discover a pause forces a re-route or brings you to a halt with a "road closed" sign. The navigation challenges inherent in the roadblocks and detours of waiting may make you feel trapped or headed in a direction you never intended to go. We learn from a re-routed journey.

Snafus Occur

Most of us approach a vacation with anticipation. Often, we create a perfect mental scene of what we expect from the journey and the destination. These mental images rarely include car trouble, flight delays, lost luggage, reservation mix-ups, illness, or inclement weather. Vacation snafus are a mini version of waiting seasons in life. Waiting implodes our plans and expectations. The ability to adapt, re-route, or accept the delay determines how well you handle the unexpected twists and turns in your journey.

Detours Provide the Scenic Route

While interstate highways get us to our destination more quickly, the trip is often monotonous. Miles of billboard-dotted roadways and dodging maniac drivers does little to make the trip pleasant. A detour usually takes you on back roads, past fruit and vegetable stands, farmhouses and fields, and through quaint towns with unique shops and stunning architecture.

Sometimes, we're so focused on getting to the destination we don't take time to notice sights along the way or stop to view something of interest. The detours waiting brings provide opportunities to build relationships, engage in endeavors that help us grow, learn something new, and find moments of relaxation, if we're willing to embrace the slower pace.

Roadblocks Provide Opportunities for Reassessment

For years, I worked out at a gym near our house, going early in the morning before sunrise. When the weather was warm, I walked to the gym, but on frigid days, I drove. My route was through a small subdivision of patio homes.

As I traveled that road one morning in the pre-dawn darkness, I came upon a makeshift roadblock and barely stopped before hitting it. The area was still under construction, and some residents cut down on thru traffic by making their own roadblock. However, they failed to include any reflective material, and several unsuspecting motorists slammed into the barricade before someone reported it to authorities and it was dismantled.

Roadblocks are annoying. The plans we made and set in motion come to a screeching halt. We're forced to stop, rethink our direction, and formulate a different plan. Even then, our plans and God's rarely align. Perhaps the roadblock that forces you to wait is God's way of slowing you and pointing you in a different direction, one that is better for you.

Roadblocks serve a purpose. Often, they protect from something dangerous ahead that isn't visible from your current location. Accept them without attempting to go around them. Stop and seek wisdom as you re-route your journey.

Eventually You Reach a Destination

Sometimes we know a waiting period is likely, but often we hit waiting when we're full speed ahead. The impact can be jarring. Waiting is hard because it changes everything from a planned course to an anticipated time frame. While waiting may cause a course correction that impacts your destination, the good news is you will eventually reach journey's end. In accepting roadblocks and detours, you reach the destination God planned for you.

Stop at the crossroads and look around. Ask for the old, godly way, and walk in it. Travel its path, and you will find rest for your souls.

Jeremiah 6:16 NLT

As you consider your pause, look for areas in your life that may need adjustment. Are you impatient, willful, self-focused, or resistant? Are you depending on yourself rather than God? Does the need for control hold you in a vise grip that keeps you awake at night? Or perhaps you are held hostage by your emotions. Do some self-assessment. Then, ponder the truth in this book as you learn to wait well.

Chapter 2

Trusting God's Time Frame

The Lord does not delay [as though He were unable to act] and is not slow about His promise, as some count slowness, but is [extraordinarily] patient toward you, not wishing for any to perish but for all to come to repentance.

2 Peter 3:9 AMP

During a beach vacation, I got up early every morning to watch the sunrise. Each sunrise was different depending on cloud cover. One day, as I waited on my balcony for the red-orange orb to appear on the horizon, I noticed a number of people sitting or standing on the shore, facing east. No one demonstrated impatience by pacing or fidgeting, nor were they glued to their cell phones. All waited, quietly, calmly, mesmerized, with faces glued to the sky.

While the weather app listed a time for sunrise, no bit of technology could predict the exact moment the first rays spilled over the lip of clouds and poured onto the sparkling surface below. Only God determined the second when anticipation became reality and light burst forth, heralding the day.

So it is with our lives as we wait for God's timing to come to fruition. The time frame God has appointed for each of us is as different as the appearance of sunrise each day. Sometimes, the timing of activities and circumstances clicks in what feels like perfect sequence to us. Other times, waiting hangs over us like thick clouds, impenetrable, obscuring the ability to see what lies ahead and understand the reason for delay. Hints of the whys of God's timing are only apparent later, or sometimes, not at all.

Waiting When Others Aren't

"We have an announcement," gushed a radiant young woman in our life group. "Well, it really may be more of a prayer request. You see, we're expecting. Again! This baby is our little oops. We already have our hands full with three children, but I guess the Lord knows what he's doing, so we'll make the best of it."

Congratulations rippled around the room. A few guys high-fived the expectant father. The mother-to-be rubbed her still-flat tummy and murmured something about hating maternity clothes.

I stared at the floor, not risking a glance at my husband, and willed myself not to cry. Emotions washed over me—sadness, anger, frustration. And then I began my internal dialogue with God.

It's not fair! They already have three children. We've waited so long and prayed so hard. All we're asking for is one baby. How long are you going to make us wait?

During a prayer, I squeezed my husband's arm, signaling my departure. Alone, leaning against the cold tile wall in the bathroom stall, I cried until I threw up.

Infertility is a gut-wrenching, emotionally charged road to travel. According to the United States Department of Health and Human Services, 6.1 million married couples in the U.S. make the journey. One of the most difficult aspects of infertility is the fact that it takes a very private, intimate part of a couple's life and makes it public.

Well-meaning friends, family members, or even complete strangers, feel it is acceptable to ask probing questions about a couple's plans for children, and level of fertility, after what they consider an acceptable time frame following the wedding.

I still remember the day I got a phone call from a friend. She began the conversation with, "A group of us moms were together and we just wondered … you want children, don't you?"

This probe was hurtful. The gathering that precipitated the question excluded me because I was not a mother, my childlessness was the conversation topic, and this type of probe was not about concern, but gossip. When you already feel left out because you're infertile, the last question you want to hear is "You do want children, don't you?"

Our journey through infertility lasted years. Until this phone call, only our families and a few close friends knew about our struggles to have a child—the tests, surgeries, disappointments, and the waiting.

During these waiting years, I navigated life in a fog because I was so self-absorbed in emotional pain. Prayers seemed to bounce off the ceiling and hit me in the face. Every pregnancy or birth announcement underscored what we were missing. I felt defective.

As with most life circumstances, hindsight is keen, and if I made the trip over again, I'd work harder to have a different perspective and trust God more.

Infertility is nothing new. Scripture mentions seven infertile couples: Abraham and Sarah, Isaac and Rebekah, Jacob and Rachel, Hannah and Elkanah, Manoah and his wife, the Shunammite woman and her husband, Elizabeth and Zachariah. They struggled with the same issues surrounding infertility that couples do today and handled the heartache of infertility in different ways.

Running Ahead of God's Timing

God's perception of time differs from ours. He sees the overall picture while we only see current circumstances. Our perception is colored by what we want to have happen and by the timing we presume makes sense. What is happening in our lives right now often determines our motivations, and actions are frequently fueled by impatience.

Infertility is one of the most challenging, and heartbreaking circumstances a couple faces, and the pain of infertility is compounded by the whispers, unsolicited advice, and questions. When waiting for a child drags on for years, and tests and procedures produce no answers, a couple either gives up hope or takes drastic steps.

The book of Genesis tells a story of infertility. Sarai (later called Sarah) was well beyond childbearing years when she went to her husband Abram (renamed Abraham) with a plan.

The Lord has prevented me from having children. Go and sleep with my servant. Perhaps I can have children through her.

Genesis 16:2 NLT

Wait. What?

Sarah's level of desperation must have been off the charts. Even though men in that culture often had more than one wife, Sarah's suggestion of using her servant as a surrogate shows how badly she wanted a child.

Abraham agreed with the plan, and out of his union with Sarah's slave, Ishmael was born. But it wasn't long before the consequences of putting a self-made plan into action instead of waiting for God's timing appeared. Scripture tells us that as soon as Hagar knew she was pregnant, she treated her mistress Sarah with contempt. Although Sarah concocted the plan, when the scheme went awry, she blamed Abraham.

Consequences of Imposing Your Timing

Taking matters into our hands always has consequences. Waiting is hard, and when circumstances seem impossible, we often opt for speeding up the process and trying to make something happen. Then, when the consequences come, we look around for someone else to blame.

Sarah took her frustrations out on Abraham, who sidestepped, and, in essence, gave her permission to abuse Hagar. Sarah treated her servant so harshly Hagar fled.

"Helping" God when timing isn't what we expect is a big mistake. And the consequences of hurrying are rarely positive.

Acceptance

> *Accept the way God does things, for who can straighten*
> *what he has made crooked?*

Ecclesiastes 7:13 NLT

Have you ever heard someone declare, "That is unacceptable!" or "I refuse to accept that!" The word "accept" has several definitions. The two that apply to waiting are "to endure without protest or reaction" and "to receive willingly." While enduring a time of waiting is likely, "without protest" and "willingly," are harder to accomplish.

Inherent in acceptance is acknowledgment of God's authority, so perhaps waiting teaches surrender of willfulness and self-sufficiency. As you wait, consider the underlying factors in your resistance to God's methods and timing. What prevents you from accepting God's way?

Often, strong-willed personalities are resistant to advice, not even willing to take the time to listen to suggestions but forging ahead with hastily-made decisions despite warnings. While it seems counterintuitive to resist Almighty God, we're often so intent on following through with our plans we ignore him.

God's Timing Serves a Purpose

He said to them, "It is not for you to know times or seasons that the Father has fixed by his own authority."

Acts 1:7 ESV

God's plans and purposes are not always evident to us. God has the advantage of seeing all the pieces of our life's puzzle with 20/20 vision, while we only see a fraction of them with distorted perception.

How many times have you been working an intricate jigsaw puzzle, been certain you found the right piece for a particular section, only to realize on closer inspection that the piece you selected doesn't quite fit? The shape seems right, the colors correct, but when you try to insert the piece, a tiny kink in the angle of one protrusion causes the piece not to fit, after all.

John 11 recounts the story of Lazarus. Mary and Martha, his sisters, sent word to Jesus that Lazarus was sick. They were Jesus' close friends, and they expected him to come immediately. Knowing his healing power, and his love for Mary, Martha, and Lazarus, Jesus' disciples were surprised when he said Lazarus' illness would not result in death and remained where he was two more days.

Then, Jesus told his disciples Lazarus had died and they were going to Bethany. The disciples were confused and concerned. Jewish leaders had attempted to stone Jesus not long before. Why would Jesus risk his life, and perhaps theirs, by going to that vicinity if he knew Lazarus was dead? If he were willing to take this kind of risk, why didn't he go two days before?

Often, we are confused by God's timing, especially when it makes little sense to us. But God always has a plan and a purpose for his time frame.

When Jesus neared Bethany, Martha ran to meet him, saying, "Lord, if you had been here, my brother would not have died" (Mark 11:21 NIV). Then Martha followed with words that expressed her faith and trust, "I know that even now God will give you whatever you ask."

Jesus delayed going to Bethany so God's glory could be revealed. Sometimes, God waits to act so the miracle is obvious.

Kathy's Story

"In January, my father died. Eight weeks later, in March, I experienced the sting of death again when my mother joined my father in heaven. 2020 marked my first Mother's Day without my mother and my first Father's Day without my father.

"Friends ask me all the time how I've had the strength to go through two major deaths within eight weeks of each other. It's mind boggling when I reflect on God's timing, but through this journey, I have gained insights on several truths about God:

- God is faithful.
- He provides.
- He instructs and shows us what we need to do.
- God gives peace to combat fear and worry.
- We have a living hope that assures me my parents are now together in heaven.
- My parents are happy, celebrating with Jesus, and wouldn't want to return to this life if they could.
- My parents' Christian legacy lives on.
- Prayer works. Countless friends prayed for me during the eight weeks surrounding my parents' passing. From these prayers, God has strengthened me and given me peace.
- God reveals himself to us.
- God blesses us.

"Although I wouldn't have chosen this timing for my parents' deaths, God has been so apparent during this time in my life. I recently created a long list to remind me of God's blessings throughout this season in my journey. Thank you, Lord, for guiding me during this season. What a joy it has been connecting God's dots and journaling his many blessings during this unique time in my life, and in history."

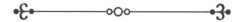

Despite the challenges of Kathy's experience, she could see God in her situation and glean the positive aspects of his time frame.

Chapter 3

Understanding God's Control

People can make all kinds of plans, but only the Lord's plan will happen.

Proverbs 19:21 NCV

Have you ever known someone who is super organized, planning each element of life down to the minutest detail? While that level of organization may give the illusion of control, it only takes one tiny glitch for the control train to derail. An unexpected event or illness, appointment change, delay, or worldwide pandemic sends the carefully orchestrated plan into a tailspin.

The unexpected forces change, and the waiting that accompanies those changes challenges our faith. We have the choice of seeing God in our circumstances or wondering if he has abandoned us.

Jeslyn's Story

"In 2012, my husband and I went through our first miscarriage. Honestly, leading up to that point in our marriage, a miscarriage wasn't a thought or even a possibility of a thought. It was so unexpected. I'm one of six children and my mom had never miscarried. My oldest sister had four children and my other sister had three children, and neither had miscarried.

"After my miscarriage, I felt so alone—alone in my thoughts, alone in my grief. Not because my mom and sisters weren't checking on me and praying for me as I walked through this season, but because none of them had ever been through what I was experiencing.

"Even my husband couldn't fully relate because it was our first pregnancy, and it was so early that I don't think he was as emotionally attached as I was. My thoughts were flooded with questions and pronouncements—Why me? Of course it would be me, what if we are never able to conceive? My body is failing us. I was on an emotional roller coaster.

"For the first time in my life, I felt my efforts were completely and utterly useless. It was hard for me to let go of control of this situation, while realizing I had zero control over any of it to begin with. It didn't matter if I ate perfectly, took every vitamin, and exercised regularly. This was the Lord's plan for us. That realization hit quickly, but the fears lingered. The what ifs wouldn't go away.

"A few months later we were blessed to get pregnant with our first healthy baby. This time, I was even more scared. What if we lost this baby, too? I was glad to know we could achieve another pregnancy, but the fear of not being able to carry to term was overwhelming. All I could do was trust God, his unknown (to us) plan for our baby, and thank Him for still being good no matter the outcome.

"During this time of uncertainty, worship helped me a lot. I've always loved singing, even as a young child, and worship songs truly speak for me. They are my prayers when I have no words. I sang 'Oceans' by Hillsong probably a thousand times in our home, in my car, as I worked. That song was my cry and anthem to God.

"Something else that helped me were the stories of others who had been through the same thing. I had no idea how common miscarriage was until ours. When I shared our experience, I heard an influx of similar stories. It was so reassuring that we weren't alone, and, even more so, that we could be understood in our grief.

"Unfortunately, our first miscarriage wasn't our last. Over the next seven years, between the births of our four healthy children the Lord is allowing us to raise, we had three additional miscarriages. Each time, I learned all over again just how little control I have. I learned the Lord gives and the Lord takes away, but still his name is to be praised. I learned I wasn't being punished for anything that I or my husband had done.

"Our journey was mapped out from the beginning. After our first miscarriage, my mom gave me a small angel painting that my cousin made. She gave me one after losing the next three babies. Now, this is something I like to do for my friends who tragically miscarry. These angel paintings are beautiful reminders of our four little souls who are in the presence of Jesus.

"This is our story, and it's what He is using to reach and help others who are experiencing a miscarriage for the first time. The most powerful evidence of Jesus we have are our personal stories and we want to share ours with others."

Jeslyn's story is one of experiencing the unexpected, feeling alone, dealing with fear, relinquishing control, and praising God in the midst of uncertainty. Sharing her story with others not only brings her comfort but also continues to minister to those who are grieving the loss of a child by miscarriage, helping them to cope and see God's faithfulness in their season of waiting.

Similar to Jeslyn's experience, some of my longest years came in the waiting room of infertility. My anxiety grew with each friend or family member who achieved a pregnancy and birthed a baby. I experienced despair, depression, and anger. My waking hours, and even my dreams, were consumed with thoughts of having a child.

Despite all the tests and procedures, I ultimately had to acknowledge the timing was out of my control. After our children were born, those waiting years rendered our children even more precious to me and provided empathy and compassion for those dealing with infertility.

Submitting to the Master's Touch

Sometimes we have the mistaken idea that once we accept Christ as Savior, we're "fixed" and don't require additional adjustments. But actually, the day we accept Christ is when the real work begins.

Because our natural tendency is toward sin and self-sufficiency, our spiritual lives are a work-in-progress. Like a lump of clay on a potter's wheel, our lives often become unbalanced, the pot a little lopsided as we spin through our daily existence. God nudges us, pushing an area back into place when he sees one side collapsing or cutting away excess when necessary. But unlike clay, we make the choice of whether we submit to these adjustments.

Mark 8:22-26 tells the story of Jesus healing a blind man and is often referred to as the story of "the second touch." When Jesus restored the man's sight, his first attempt wasn't totally complete. While the man could see, people looked like trees. Only after Jesus applied an additional touch could the man see clearly.

An interesting aspect of this story is the blind man aiding Jesus in his healing by telling him what his vision was like after the first touch. If the blind man hadn't been honest about his vision, he may have gone through the rest of his life with only partially restored sight. But because he told Jesus what he saw, and allowed a second touch from the master, his sight was fully restored.

We need the Master's touch, but often we bat his hand aside and opt for someone else's touch, the input of friends or looking for answers online. We're given the opportunity to assist in our spiritual development, but often don't. We become self-sufficient, thinking we know best.

Reasons We Need the Master's Touch

We're conformers. It's easy to get sidetracked on our spiritual journey. The world bombards us with influences that mold and shape us into someone different from what God intends. We listen to other voices and compromise attitudes and actions. At first, we feel a little guilty; then not so much. Friends, activities, or love relationships take first place in our lives and soon we're not communicating with the Father. We naturally drift toward worldly thinking and actions, making us need God's corrective touch. But often we run from it.

We're impatient. Many times, we tire of waiting for God to act. We pray, and He doesn't answer; or answers in a way we don't like. So we make decisions that send us in a direction different from the one God has planned for our lives. Impatience robs us of gifts God has in store for us.

We're near-sighted. Most of us need spiritual glasses. We see only what is happening right now and focus on the feelings we have at this moment. But God's view is far-sighted. He knows the course of our lives from before our birth until after our death. His vision is always 20/20. Our sight often requires a second, third, or fourth touch from the Master before we see clearly.

We're sometimes blind. Often, we miss the obvious. God speaks and we fail to listen, so he waves red flags to snag our attention, warning us away from people or situations that are dangerous. But we slip on the dark glasses and ignore Him. We create our blindness and then sidestep Him when he reaches out to touch our eyes, swiping the cloudiness from our vision.

Allow God to be Hands-On

The catalyst for submission is confession. But we blame others when our actions—what we fail to do or what we do willfully—go against God's laws. Somehow, we're blind to our responsibility, even when we see the consequences for our decisions. In confessing, we admit responsibility and restore our connection and relationship to God.

Accept His Re-Shaping Touch

If you've ever had braces on your teeth, or had a broken bone reset, you know there is pain involved in re-alignment. Submitting to spiritual re-shaping brings a similar discomfort. It's hard to view the sin in our lives. Instead, we compare ourselves to others and adopt an attitude that says, I'm not as bad as this person or that person. But sin is sin, and anything, even pride, separates us from God. It's painful to look at facets of our lives that are out of line with God's commandments, but unless we're willing to see and acknowledge areas of sin, and allow God to re-shape us, we're living lives outside His will.

*But the pot he was shaping from the clay was marred
in his hands; so the potter formed it into another pot,
shaping it as seemed best to him.*

Jeremiah 18:4 NIV

Trust His Vision

We all have dreams of how we want our lives to go. We imagine various scenarios and then expect God to go along with our plans. But Proverbs 16:9 says, "We make our own plans, but the Lord decides where we will go" (CEV). We avoid a lot of frustration and heartache if we entrust our dreams, and our lives, to God and ask for his wisdom and input before deciding and taking action.

Often, when it feels like God is taking too long to answer our prayers, we move forward without waiting to hear from him. Trust is an important part of our faith walk, but sometimes we trust others, or ourselves, more than we trust God. It's incredibly foolish to do this considering God's infinite power and omniscient wisdom. By acknowledging you are not in control, and trusting God, you gain wide-screen vision. Submit to his healing, reshaping touch and enjoy the benefits.

Jay's Story–Waiting for the Fulfillment of a Dream

"I've always loved music, and ever since high school, I've also loved recording music. I never thought it would become my job, but in college, a friend wrote an article about me for a communications project. When he interviewed me, he asked a question that was the first spark of my studio dream—'Do you think you'll ever have your own studio?' I smiled and replied something like, 'That would be really cool,' not thinking it was a realistic goal.

"After graduating from college in 2012, I joined the music staff at our church, where my passion for recording and music production continued to grow. I remember once telling a staff friend, in a defeated tone, that I wished I could have a studio like a big one we knew of in North Carolina where many of our favorite artists recorded. At that point, I still didn't think it was a realistic goal.

"Relatively soon after that, the dream seemed to become more tangible. In 2014, my wife and I were members of a newlywed Bible study group, and one evening during prayer request time, Chelsea and I shared I felt like I was supposed to have a studio at some point—a 'real studio' in a commercial building somewhere. We didn't know what to say other than that.

"Thankfully, God allowed Greenbriar Studio to become my full-time job on Christmas Day 2015, working from my home. By 2016, the vision had grown, and the location for a stand-alone studio narrowed to Greenville, SC.

"I was ready to go that very moment, but it wasn't time yet. I read *The Circle Maker* by Mark Batterson and was on a faith high for weeks, imagining the studio vision could happen any second. When it didn't, I crashed and was so discouraged I tried to avoid the thought of a big studio for months. I didn't want to get my hopes up again.

"Fast forward to July 2020, the big studio, 'Greenbriar 2.0' as I like to call it, has not been built or even officially designed, but we have moved to Greenville, the anticipated location. I am currently praying around a piece of land I feel I was led to for building the studio. I also now realize God has been, and still is, teaching me and preparing me to be a good steward of the dream before it is realized.

Listening

"I've known how to pray for most of my life, but I didn't start learning to listen for God's voice until 2016. Inspired by a few of my worship leader friends, one morning, I sat alone at the kitchen table in silence, with my eyes closed and hands open. I wanted guidance and clarity specifically for the recording studio vision, but I asked God to just tell me something. Anything.

"I don't know how much time passed or how many transient thoughts filtered through my mind as I waited, not even knowing exactly what I was waiting for. Then, suddenly, the phrase 'forgive him,' along with the name of a former coworker, came to my mind. I had neither thought about nor talked to this person in a considerable amount of time. I was reluctant to follow through, and it took me several days to do so. I emailed my former coworker and told him I forgave him for words and actions that had hurt me. As I was writing the email, I also apologized for my actions and words..

"Since then, in times of discouragement or busyness, I have often failed to take time to listen to God. But recently my passion for listening and waiting for God's voice has been renewed, knowing that I desperately need his guidance—not only for the studio dream, but for everyday life and my walk with Him.

The Present

"Having a big dream for the future has often made it hard for me to keep my eyes off the horizon and pay attention to what is right under my nose. I have a beautiful wife and two amazing young children. It has unfortunately been easy for me to slip into daydreams or discouraged slumps when thinking of the future while my family is trying to spend quality time with me. God opened my eyes to this, and I have recently had some of the best, undistracted quality time with my family. Being with and making memories with them is far more important than trying to discern the next step for my business.

"This concept extends beyond my family and inspires me to be on the lookout for divine appointments throughout a normal day. It's easy to focus on the to-do list and block everything else out, but God may have appointments in store for me that directly affect the studio's future. I am learning to be present and flexible with my schedule.

Anxiety

"'Anxiety' and 'anxious' were words I had heard many times in my life, but I did not truly understand their meaning until 2017. When our first child, Emerald, was a newborn, my wife was recovering from a C-section. Since she needed to stay at the house, it was up to me, a new dad, to take Emerald for her first checkup all by myself. My mind began spiraling out of control.

"My sister was visiting at our house when it was near time for me to leave for the doctor with Emerald. I felt an emotional tension in my chest and explained what I was thinking: 'If I go by myself and the nurses ask questions about Emerald's birth or how many diapers she's had changed today, or how much she has eaten, or family history questions about who has had what diseases and on what side, I'm going to either forget the correct answers or not know the answers, and I'm going to look like a stupid, stereotypical caveman husband who has no business taking care of a child.'

"I was completely overcome and paralyzed by the irrational fear of countless scenarios that played out in my imagination. My sister simply responded, 'That's anxiety,' and kindly asked if I wanted her to come with us to the appointment. I took her up on the offer.

"In the wake of that day, God helped me realize how many times I had felt those same kinds of feelings in different situations all the way back to my childhood. I did not know how to verbalize those feelings, and I didn't know there was any point in verbalizing them. As much as I tried to live out 1 Peter 5:7, 'Cast all your anxiety on him because he cares for you', I usually couldn't *snap out of it.*

"In July of 2020 after a group Bible study on anxiety, something changed. I was a few days into reading *Draw the Circle* by Mark Batterson and praying over the new studio location and building. On July 27, I felt a nervous chest tension (a fairly regular occurrence) sometime that morning. Instead of letting the feeling grow, I took a deep breath, thought a quick prayer in the vein of I give it to you, God, felt the tension release, and moved on with my morning. God broke through my typical spirals as they began and reminded me to cast my cares on Him. I repeated this process several times that week.

"I'm confident this give-it-to-God mindset has now become a habit for me, and I believe it is an essential change he made in my heart to prepare me for what is coming. I believe I am about to see an expensive, potentially stressful dream come true. I cannot be a successful, responsible steward of this gift if I allow fear and anxiety to drive my thoughts and actions. My faith is increasing as my worry decreases. No matter how long I have to wait to see the studio dream fulfilled, I am forever thankful for the changes God is making in my life and how he is teaching me along the way."

Chapter 4

Praying While Waiting

Don't worry about anything; instead, pray about everything. Tell God what you need, and thank him for all he has done. Then you will experience God's peace, which exceeds anything we can understand. His peace will guard your hearts and minds as you live in Christ Jesus.

Philippians 4:6-7 NLT

Temper means to attune or to bring to a suitable state by mixing or adding ingredients. A good tempering makes a product (or a person) stronger and more resilient through hardship. Prayer does all of that. Prayer brings us into harmony with God and adds to and changes our perception. Prayer toughens and strengthens us for difficult life situations and for times when God allows seasons of waiting.

Tempered glass is a type of safety glass that is toughened by thermal or chemical treatments to make it stronger than ordinary glass. If tempered glass breaks, it fractures into small, potentially less harmful, pieces. Prayer tempers waiting, helping us break the waiting into manageable sections, and gain greater perspective.

> "We tend to use prayer as a last resort, but God wants it to be our first line of defense. We pray when there's nothing else we can do, but God wants us to pray before we do anything at all."
>
> **~Oswald Chambers**

Let Prayer Be Your First Go-To While Waiting

One day, I dashed into a store to purchase a single item. It took several minutes for me to locate what I was looking for and decide. Then I headed for the checkout counter. As I reached the end of the aisle and rounded the corner, I stopped short. Fifteen people stood in line for a single checker. No big deal, I thought. She'll call for help and get this line moving. But there was no call for backup support, and nearly twenty minutes later, I was still waiting to check out.

When waiting, the normal tendency is to find an activity to fill time, giving the perception of accomplishing something so the delay won't feel so long. If you're in a waiting room, you read, talk to a companion or stranger, or people-watch. When standing in line, you count floor tiles, peruse items you don't need that are placed along the line to entice buyers, scan social media or read emails on your phone, commiserate with bystanders, listen to conversations around you, check the time to see how long you've been in line, or create if-then scenarios—if I'm not to the turn in the line in five minutes, I'm leaving.

Prayer is not high on the list, or even on the list, of activities to engage in while waiting. Prayer doesn't come naturally for most of us because it's not something we've learned to value. Often, our focus is on doing what it takes to get beyond a waiting period, but prayer is saved for a point of desperation.

Ideally, prayer should be an ongoing conversation with God, as easily engaged in as a conversation with a trusted friend. However, often we haven't cultivated a relationship with God to the level we experience the type of freedom to make him our first go-to source. Other times, we avoid prayer because we know we need to come clean with God about an area of our lives that isn't in harmony with his directives. But it is possible to overcome barriers and cultivate the type of prayer routine that becomes a normal and natural part of life.

A Life of Prayer

When one of my aunts was near the end of her life, my husband, son, his fiancée, and I went to see her in the care facility. When I had been to see my aunt the week before, she dozed most of the time I was there. But this day, she was awake and aware. We talked for a while, and then my aunt suddenly said, "Let's pray." I assumed she wanted us to pray for her, but before any of us could pray, she launched into a heartfelt prayer. Her weak voice took on a tone of authority and strength as she praised God for his faithfulness to her and our family and then prayed for each of us.

When she finished praying, we kissed her goodbye. As we walked down the hall, I told my son and his fiancée they had just witnessed the prayer of someone who had walked with the Lord a long time and had cultivated a relationship and communication with God that many never experience. This type of example encourages the pursuit of a vibrant prayer life.

Prayer Opens Doors

Acts 16:25-26 records the amazing story of Paul and Silas and the power of prayer to change circumstances. Jailed and bound with chains, Paul and Silas had little hope of escape. Yet, even in this depressing situation, they prayed and sang praises to God.

Their reaction sets a powerful example of how we should respond when we are bound in a time of waiting. Paul and Silas did not give in to despondency, hopelessness, or anger. Instead, they prayed and praised God, and the other prisoners listened. As Paul and Silas prayed, God caused an earthquake that flung open the doors and broke the chains of all those in the prison.

God has the power to answer your prayers in an equally dramatic way, to change your circumstances or help you navigate your season of waiting.

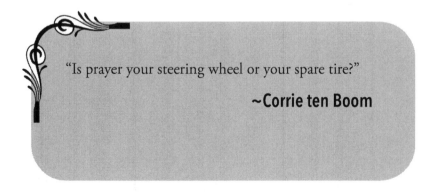

"Is prayer your steering wheel or your spare tire?"

~Corrie ten Boom

Prayer Lessons

People have various views regarding prayer. For some, prayer is merely a head bob or an eyebrow scratch, a few words at mealtime, or something they resort to when facing a difficult situation. For others, it is an integral part of daily life.

Prayer is a privilege afforded us as children of God. It's an invitation to approach our Heavenly Father with praise, thanksgiving, confession, and requests. Prayer allows us to gain comfort, wisdom, direction, and peace. We handicap ourselves when we fumble through life without the benefits of prayer. God is available. He loves us, knows our needs, desires a relationship with us, and wants us to interact with him.

Jesus instructed his followers in effective prayer. Assess your prayers and then implement elements from Jesus' example.

Make Forgiveness a Priority

Have you witnessed a marriage or friendship that fell apart and wondered why? Often, the root of broken relationships is tied to an offense or perceived offense, failing to forgive, and a dose of stubbornness thrown in to ensure reconciliation never happens.

Forgiveness is the main tenant of Christianity, yet many of us cannot bring ourselves to forgive those who hurt us. Failure to forgive erects a barrier between us and God. There is great irony in asking God to forgive our sins, and expecting him to hear and answer, while we refuse to forgive the sins of others. (Luke 11:4)

Acknowledge God's Authority and Power

When Jesus taught his disciples to pray, he began by acknowledging God's holiness and position of authority. In doing so, we maintain the reverence God deserves and recognize where we stand in relation to him. (Luke 11:2)

Cultivate Private Prayer

Not long ago, I cleaned out the carport storage room at my childhood home and found my father's carpenter's tool chest. Growing up, I often walked construction sites with my father and learned lessons about building, like the need for a sturdy and level foundation and using the right tools for the job. Mingled with construction lessons were life lessons such as the importance of building a firm, level spiritual foundation through prayer.

One of my fondest memories of my father was seeing him at our kitchen table early in the morning with open Bible, folded hands, and head bowed in prayer. Just like the tools in his contractor's tool belt, prayer had a well-worn handle. My father knew the power of prayer and modeled personal prayer for me.

Prayer is one of the greatest resources in our spiritual tool chest, yet one we often leave underutilized until we encounter difficult situations—a season of waiting, a frightening diagnosis, a natural disaster, or some other type of life-altering event. We deny ourselves the gift of prayer because we mistakenly think we should be able to work out life's problems on our own.

Jesus is our greatest example of the importance of prayer. He often slipped away in the early morning hours for time alone with his father. Luke 6:12 tells us Jesus went off to the mountain to pray and spent the night in prayer to God. Other verses reinforce Jesus' practice of separating himself from others so he could spend time alone with the Father in prayer. This exemplifies the high priority we should also give prayer.

When we pray publicly, we pray more formally. But prayers that happen when we are alone with God often come from deep places within. We confess sins, express fears, and admit hurts. Private prayers bring cleansing and healing. These prayers can be spoken or written in the pages of a journal. Private prayer prepares us for the day, or for sleep, and brings us closer to the Father. (Matthew 6:6)

Confess with Honesty and Humility

Often, we approach confession with the attitude that if we don't tell God, he won't know what we've done. But nothing is hidden from his view. He knows our sin, and pretending something didn't happen only amplifies the separation sin causes between us and God.

Pride is a big issue for most of us, and confessing with honesty and humility requires practice. But the more we are honest with God, the easier it becomes, and as our love grows for the Father, the less we want to disappoint him. We think before we make choices we know will cause him sorrow. (Luke 18:13-14)

Pray about Everything

Sometimes we have the mistaken idea that we should just handle situations without involving God. Perhaps we think these issues are too small to bother him with or that we should be capable enough to take care of them ourselves, but Jesus instructed us to pray about everything. (Luke 11:9)

Ask for Needs

God knows our needs, but acknowledging needs and asking for help strengthens our relationship with God and keeps the father-child relationship in perspective. (John 16:24)

While it is fine to pray for your needs and those of others, don't approach God with a shopping list of requests. Praise him. Thank him, before the answer to prayer and afterwards, and keep in mind he is the source of every good gift. (James 1:17)

Pray in Jesus' Name

Praying in Jesus' name taps into his power and position with God the Father. The name of Jesus is powerful, and the Holy Spirit translates our prayers into better verbiage than we could ever construct on our own.

> *Very truly I tell you, my Father will give you whatever you ask in my name.*

> John 16:23 NIV

Exercise Bold Persistence in Prayer

Jesus provided examples of persistent prayer: a man continually knocking at the door until it opened (Luke 11:8-10) and a widow who did not give up in her plea for justice (Luke 18:4).

In recent years, I've learned lessons about persistent prayer. I prayed for almost two years for a family member who was making unwise decisions and prayed for over five years for the sale of a rental house. During those years, I often felt God was not listening. There were times when I was angry with God (and told him so) because there was not even a hint of answers.

Sometimes, I stopped praying for periods of time, but then Scripture, the words of a sermon, or the wisdom of Christian friends snapped me back to the importance of praying with boldness and persistence. Just when I was about to give up, God dramatically answered one request and then the other.

While you are waiting for God to answer your prayers, don't give up. God's silence isn't inattention or failure to answer, but his answer is sometimes "no" or "wait."

Cultivating an Effective Prayer Life

Jesus showed us, by his example, the importance of prayer. A vibrant prayer life is exciting and life-changing. If prayer isn't a standard practice for you, or if the importance you placed on prayer has waned, consider cultivating or revitalizing a prayer life.

Pave the Way

One afternoon, as I worked in our sun room, I heard a noise outside, a low rumble that seemed to increase in intensity. We live in a flight path for the airport, so I thought it might be a low-flying cargo plane, but as the noise grew louder and closer, a vibration accompanied the sound. Soon, the vibration rattled dishes. Our area of the state experiences mild earthquakes from time to time, but this was different.

Finally, the noise and vibration were so intense I went to the front door and looked out. A giant machine crept up the street. After it passed, I saw it was making striations in the pavement with a claw-like apparatus.

A few days later, a truck filled potholes with gravel, while another truck followed spraying cracks with tar. Several weeks later, a crew resurfaced our street with blacktop. If the crew hadn't prepared the road first, the new surface would have been less likely to stick.

Paving the way for prayer is similar. If you take time to prepare, the habit of prayer has a better chance of sticking.

Determine a Set Time

Prayer is more likely to happen if you designate a set time and give it priority. Consider the feasibility of the time you set. While morning is good, is a morning prayer time actually doable for you? If you wake up easily and can get up earlier and have a time of prayer, go with morning. If you have difficulty waking up every day and are more alert at night, choose evening.

Consider the time you set as a standing appointment and observe it as you do other appointments. It may take several weeks to form a prayer habit (some studies say it takes 30 days to form a habit), but if you follow the practice each day, you will look forward to this time with God.

Have a Plan

While you don't want to hold to such a rigid structure that you don't allow God to lead in a different direction, create a loose framework for your time of prayer. The A.C.T.S. (Adoration, Confession, Thanksgiving, Supplication) acrostic, or something similar, lends structure to prayer. Find what works well for you, but allow yourself some flexibility if an urgent request or need for in-depth confession requires most of your allotted time.

Embrace Quietness

Each day, we are bombarded by noise and distractions. People often have the TV on even when no one is in the room watching or listening. And most of us turn on the radio, or listen to books on tape or a podcast while in the car.

A friend told me once that he made it a practice to turn off the radio in the car so he could pray. "I know I'm avoiding God when I get in the car and turn on the radio," he said.

While multi-tasking may feel productive, prayer needs your total attention. Quietness allows you to focus and hear God's voice.

Listen

Our three-year-old grandson thoroughly embraces his independence. Often, that independence excludes listening and obedience. To underscore the need to listen, my daughter pretends to put on "listening ears" and asks our grandson to do the same.

Often, we talk more than we listen in life and in prayer. However, to get the most out of prayer, cultivate listening. God speaks via many avenues. Recognizing his voice requires ears that listen well and a heart and mind that comprehend.

Pray Honestly

I grew up hearing the phrase "honesty is the best policy" and that applies to your prayer life as well. God doesn't want some elaborate phraseology or repeated mantra, he wants honesty and relationship. Pray with transparency and humility. Be honest about feelings and fears. Ask for wisdom and discernment.

Shift Your Focus Outward

Look beyond yourself and your circumstances to the situations of others. Pray for them. Help, when possible. In looking at the situations of others, you get a clearer picture of your own. Realize you are not the only one in a holding pattern, waiting for resolution and the ability to move forward. Looking outward provides a broader perspective.

Keep a Prayer Journal

Recording prayers in a journal is an effective way of keeping track of requests. Journaling also helps you express concerns, record praises, and remain focused during prayer. When you receive answers to prayers, remember to thank God, returning to the request and noting the time frame and how God answered. You will be amazed as you trace God's answers and his timing. Accept the season you are in and give thanks for the lessons God is teaching you.

Leave Your Requests with God

One of the greatest challenges of praying effectively is leaving our requests with God and trusting him for the timing of answers. In our humanness, we want an immediate response and grow restless when answers aren't forthcoming. We worry, instead of allowing God to work out situations in his way and his timing.

Ask Big, Believe Bigger, Expect Answers

In the morning Lord, you hear my voice; in the morning I lay my requests before you and wait expectantly.

Psalm 5:3 NIV

Often, when we pray, we don't really expect anything to happen. We go through the motions, as if by rote, yet lack the faith to believe God has the power to change our situation. But God encourages praying big.

Ask of Me, and I will surely give the nations as your inheritance, And the very end of the earth as Your possession.

Psalm 2:8 NASB

When you pray, believe God is going to answer. Praying with a negative attitude indicates a lack of trust in God's ability and faithfulness. Pray with persistence, expectancy, and thankfulness for what God is going to do. Even if prayer doesn't immediately change your situation, it can change your perspective.

Avoid falling into the habit of not praying about something because you think it is too outlandish for God to answer. His ability is far greater than our imagining.

Prayer Tips

1. **Redeem time.** Sometimes we have the mistaken idea that all conditions must be perfect before we can engage in a time of prayer. But one of the beautiful qualities about prayer is it can happen anywhere and any time. Have you ever awakened in the middle of the night and tried to go back to sleep without success? The longer you are awake, the more frustrated you become. Instead of fighting wakefulness, consider this a time to pray. God may even bring a specific situation or person to mind. Once you have prayed, you may find sleep returns. Other moments to redeem time may come while waiting during your day in a drive-thru or checkout line, or while waiting for someone to arrive for a meeting. Look for ways you can redeem time in your schedule and utilize these moments for prayer.

2. **Use a reminder to prompt you to pray.** Our pastor asks us to pray at a certain time each day for a specific event in the life of our church, during Holy Week, or for a person, ministry, or situation. If remembering to pray is a challenge for you, try setting a reminder on your phone.

3. **Follow an outline.** A guideline focuses your thoughts.

4. **Pray aloud.** Verbalizing your prayers has a powerful effect that often leads you into a time of praise and worship. If praying aloud intimidates you, write your prayers and then read them aloud. Reading your prayers may start teaching you to pray aloud.

5. **Wait and listen.** Often, we pray and then dash on to the next thing on our to-do list. If you are praying in a car, you probably don't have time to pull to the side of the road and ponder, but you can aid listening by turning off the radio and ignoring your phone for a period. God often speaks at unusual times and in unusual places, so be aware and tuned in for his voice.

When God is Silent

The Old Testament recounts numerous instances of God speaking directly and clearly to people. God initially spoke to Moses via a burning bush, followed by directives on what to say to Pharaoh to precipitate the release of the Israelites, and then regularly during the forty-year journey to the Promised Land. Moses received clear instructions. When he failed to carry out those instructions as directed, he experienced consequences. Likewise, when he adhered exactly to God's message, he experienced God's power.

Prophets spoke God's word to the people. When God gave a message to prophets, it often came with the directive to proclaim the message exactly as stated, without adding or subtracting words or meaning.

Yet, when we are sidetracked in a waiting period, it sometimes seems as if God is silent. When we don't receive answers to prayer, we pray less, reasoning prayer is pointless. But while you are waiting, pray more, not less. God sometimes withholds answers because our motivation is faulty or because unconfessed sin has erected a wall.

Take some time to assess anything that may block you from receiving answers to prayer. Are you holding a grudge against someone? Do you stubbornly refuse to forgive someone for a long-ago offense? Or perhaps God is speaking, but you reject what he says because you don't like the message.

Other times, God's silence is for purposes we do not understand.

Mae Frances's Story

"During a three-month period, five doctors tried to determine what was wrong with me. My symptoms included yellowing of the eyes and skin, severe itching, and extremely elevated blood enzymes. All my signs and symptoms pointed to a stone in my common bile duct.

"A surgeon planned to perform a simple procedure to remove the stone, but a test did not verify the existence of a stone. He sent me to a larger hospital for more extensive testing, but those tests also showed no evidence of a stone. I was distraught.

"When I saw the surgeon again, he was baffled. I lost thirteen pounds, my blood levels continued to climb, and my condition worsened. My local doctor thought I would not live past three weeks.

"As a nurse, not having a diagnosis, and doctors not being able to help me, weighed me down. I experienced discouragement and hopelessness. Mentally, I began preparing to die. I was too tired and weak to have hoped I would live.

"My family doctor obtained an appointment for me with a renowned specialist. His testing showed no stone or cancer. Cancer! I didn't realize until that report that I was also being tested for cancer. Had I known, I would probably have been even more discouraged. The specialist sent me to his colleague. The test he performed resulted in no definitive diagnosis. My weight continued to drop, and blood enzyme levels got higher.

"I prayed through the entire ordeal, but God was silent. I thought the end of my life was near until I remembered God's promises about what I would accomplish for His kingdom before leaving earth. I wondered if I had misunderstood Him. Then, the Sunday before I was to see a new gastroenterologist on Monday, God's voice awakened me, 'I will heal you without medication.'

"Monday at the gastroenterologist's office, my blood levels were the same as the previous week, and I had only lost a pound. The gastroenterologist wanted to wait seven more days before doing treatment, despite my complaint with itching. Since he didn't know exactly what he was dealing with, he was scared to give me anything. I smiled, remembering what God told me. I knew I would live.

"Seven days later, my enzymes dropped twenty points. My weight remained the same. Over the next twenty-one days my blood enzymes decreased five hundred points, and I gained two pounds. The healing process was in full swing, without medication.

"Ultimately, I received a diagnosis of medication-induced hepatitis, a rare side effect of an antibiotic I took for a respiratory infection three weeks before the jaundice appeared. Eventually, my levels returned to normal, the itching stopped, and I gained weight. Although the waiting was hard, physically and mentally, God was faithful and healed me without medication.

"During my illness, I didn't have the strength to read my Bible, but I could pray. My family's love and support meant a lot. My grandchildren were afraid of me because of the changes in my body. I wanted to get well for my grandchildren. I didn't want their last memory of me to be fear.

"For me, the worst part of my time of waiting was not hearing from God for so long. I wondered if I had done something to make God stop talking to me. I knew if God didn't move, my illness would end my life. God's promise to me that morning restored my hope.

"During my season of waiting, I learned I was not in control of myself, and my suffering was not for me, but for the glory of God. I learned what appears to be the obvious answer is not always true. God does not always speak the way He has in the past, and I need to trust His timing, not mine. God is faithful to do what He said he will do. I still marvel at His ways. I trust Him.

"I have shared my waiting period, and lessons I learned, with others as encouragement and comfort, as they are going through their trials."

Mae Frances's life pause involved health issues that confounded doctors and left her hopeless. One of her greatest challenges was feeling cut off from God because she could not hear his voice.

Your struggle may be the same. Sometimes the voices we hear loudest in times of waiting are those tinged with fear, doubt, and confusion.

Like my young grandson, you may need to put on "listening ears," tune out voices that distract and discourage, and attune your mind and heart to God's voice.

Chapter 5

Praising Despite the Wait

Praise the LORD! For it is good to sing praises to our God; for it is pleasant, and a song of praise is fitting.

Psalm 147:1 ESV

Our three-year-old granddaughter and grandson love to sing the blessing. Even at this young age, they know they need to wait to eat until we thank God for the food. As we fold our hands and bow our heads, they begin singing, "Thank you, God. Thank you, God, for our food."

As the song progresses, they speed up. As we near "amen," they get louder until they fairly shout "AMEN," which is then followed by resounding applause. The applause is almost longer than the blessing. Even the youngest grandson, barely a year old, joins his pudgy hands together, bounces, and smiles.

I'm not sure when applause was added to the blessing. Maybe we clapped the first time they sang all the way through the song without help. Or maybe they applaud simply in praise to God. No matter what prompts the clapping, I hope they are always this excited about offering thanksgiving and praise to God in song and words.

Choosing Praise

During the years my aunt was in a skilled care facility, she enjoyed listing to praise music. She had been a choir member for decades, and now, almost blind and confined to a wheelchair, listening to music brought her joy.

A Brooklyn Tabernacle Choir tape that included the song "Hallelujah Anyhow" was among her favorites. This upbeat, gospely song was a little wild for my aunt's usual musical taste, but the lyrics chronicle God's faithfulness and goodness no matter what comes. I believe the words resonated with her in her situation and allowed her to focus on praise rather than the bleakness of her circumstances.

Our natural bent in life's waiting rooms is to fidget, complain, pace, and grumble, so choosing to praise is a decision of resolve, one that does not always come easily.

The prophet Habakkuk paints a dismal picture of potential circumstances, but then makes the unexpected turn of praising.

Even if the fig tree does not bloom and the vines have no grapes, even if the olive tree fails to produce and the fields yield no food, even if the sheep pen is empty and the stalls have no cattle—even then, I will be happy with the Lord. I will truly find joy in God who saves me.

Habakkuk 3:17-18 GW

Praise Changes Your Perspective

The focus in these verses in Habakkuk 3 is salvation. The Children of Israel were backwards-looking whiners. They spent a lot of time complaining about what they didn't have and wishing for a return to their former existence. (Apparently, they forgot about the abuse and oppression of slavery!) But perhaps the real impetus for the grumbling was frustration over the fact that the trip to the Promised Land was taking far longer than anyone anticipated. Waiting, or traveling in a circuitous route as the Israelites were, is hard. They longed for stability, and perhaps a life that didn't involve constantly moving.

The ability to praise despite life circumstances, despite the "even ifs," revolves around focus. Praise shifts your focus from self to God. Instead of thinking about your situation, praise refocuses to God's power, plans, and purposes. Rather than whining about a time of waiting, praise zeros in on gratitude for God's provision. Praise honors and blesses God, who is worthy of praise. But praise also changes you and how you respond when life doesn't fit your time frame.

While praise can be spontaneous, we sometimes fail to praise when circumstances are difficult. Sometimes praise must be intentional. Cultivate the habit of praise, and to do that, you may need to refocus your perspective.

Finding Perspective

Weather permitting, I enjoy sitting on our deck after my morning walk. I'm in the habit of turning my chair toward the left, but the view in that direction isn't ideal. I see a bare patch where a dead tree once stood, the remnants of weeds at the edge of the woods, and unsightly stacks of empty plastic flowerpots and a neglected car in my neighbor's driveway.

One morning, I was unsettled and distracted by ongoing concerns. Without really thinking about it, I swiveled my chair toward the opposite side of the yard. I saw new foliage bursting from barren limbs. A gentle breeze stirred the branches and a hawk glided high overhead.

My other neighbor's yard stretched before me like a green carpet freckled with dappled sunlight. Cardinals danced on the deck railing and swooped to the roof. As I reflected on the different view on this side of the yard, the Lord whispered, "You need to view challenges from a new perspective."

Many situations in our lives could benefit from a new outlook. Here are some new perspectives for your time of waiting:

View Perspective from a Different Angle

In art, perspective is a technique which creates space and depth for a three-dimensional look on a flat, two-dimensional surface.

In art history courses in college, I remember being intrigued by the art of Andre Mantegna, who painted from a worm's-eye perspective. When you look at his paintings, you feel as if you are on the ground looking up.

Often, your perspective is at its lowest when you face an ongoing life challenge, or you're sidelined in a season of waiting. Perspective is colored by current circumstances, and frustration, self-pity, and impatience frequently cloud our vision.

In the 20th century, many artists began painting from a bird's-eye view. The aerial view provided a different perspective.

Sometimes, you need a broader point of reference on your situation. You need to change lenses on the camera you've been using. Instead of taking snapshots, a panoramic view is required. Often, you can't gain perspective without a wider view of your situation. It may take only one tweak of your viewfinder to adjust your point of view.

Focus Beyond Self

Recently, I have become increasingly aware of those facing serious health situations. Young men in their twenties, a childhood friend, her daughter, and others, all dealing with cancer. When I think of these people and their families, struggles I face seem minimal juxtaposed against those situations. Yet it's not unusual to get bogged down with your personal problems, afflictions, and frustrations and allow your perspective to skew in a negative direction.

Looking outward, with compassion and concern for others, and their difficulties, alters your perspective. Make praying for others part of your daily routine. Praise God for what he is going to do in their situation, and yours. Then look for ways to support and encourage others. Your insights may be beneficial, bringing new perspective to those in need. Conversely, others may bless you with fresh perceptions.

Find Hidden Gems and Express Gratitude

So often, I've seen those going through deep waters weather the storm by looking for hidden gems in their situations, expressing gratitude despite their circumstances, and taking each day as it comes, without trying to guess what tomorrow holds.

Someone dear to me has been battling cancer for seven years, yet he never complains. Recently, disease progression required advancing to more aggressive treatment. For many, this would signal cause for alarm, but he views it positively, thanking God for ongoing research and new forms of treatment that enable him to keep doing the work God called him to do.

It's difficult to find anything positive in current circumstances, but when you search and find that nugget, it's like a precious jewel gleaming amid rough stone. The quality and beauty of jewels isn't always evident in the mining process. Only later, after cleaning, cutting, and polishing by a master craftsman, is a gem's quality assessed and beauty revealed. Look for the gems in your season of waiting. Place them in a setting that enhances their value in your circumstances and praise God for the encouragement they bring.

Rest in God's Plan for Your Future

One of the biggest challenges of the life of faith is resting in God's plan and timing for your future. It shouldn't be hard because God repeatedly proves his faithfulness. Yet we struggle, trying to figure out solutions rather than believing God works out circumstances for our good. No matter how hard we try, we can't impose our time frame on the future. Instead, rest in God's plan and provision.

> *These troubles and sufferings of ours are quite small and won't last very long. Yet this short time of distress will result in God's richest blessing upon us forever and ever! So we do not look at what we can see right now, the troubles all around us, but we look forward to the joys in heaven which we have not yet seen. The troubles will soon be over, but the joys to come will last forever.*

2 Corinthians 4:17-18 TLB

Cultivate a Thankful Heart While You Wait

Years ago, I traveled to New Mexico to teach at a writing conference. As is often the case, I met some interesting people along the way. On one leg of my flight, I talked to my seatmate, sharing a little of the challenges our family faced during the past year and my thankfulness despite circumstances.

The woman beside me swiveled toward me and said, "Wait a minute. Both your mother and mother-in-law died, and your son had a severe injury and two major surgeries. How can you be thankful for any of that?"

Many times, gratitude makes little sense to those unfamiliar with the habit of thankfulness and praise, even in times of difficulty. Based on the story of the ten lepers in Luke 17, since just one of the ten returned to thank Jesus for healing, we can assume probably only a tenth of us attempt to express gratitude. But Scripture instructs something different.

> *Rejoice always, pray continually, give thanks in all circumstances; for this is God's will for you in Christ Jesus.*

> 1 Thessalonians 5:16-18 NIV

The Refining Process of Gratitude

To refine means to improve something by removing substances from it or by changing to it. An attitude of gratitude doesn't just happen. Our natural bent is often toward finding fault, seeing imperfections, and commenting on people or circumstances that annoy or displease us. But if you allow it, focusing on gratitude molds, shapes, and changes your outlook. Gratitude refines.

Gratitude Diminishes Self Pity

All of us experience difficult seasons in life. You may deal with an ongoing health issue, financial instability, significant relationship struggles, unrealized dreams, or other waiting situations that make it easy to slip into an attitude of self-pity. Being grateful diminishes feelings of self-pity.

Gratitude Improves Relationships

As previously mentioned, often we tend to zero in on habits or personality traits in others that annoy us, and sometimes we're quick to point those out. Instead, look for the good in others and what you are grateful for in your relationships. Gratitude enhances empathy and helps you overlook hurts and wrongs.

Gratitude Moves you Forward

Ingratitude holds us captive. I see social media posts from the same people that are always negative—a criticism of government officials, faith leaders, or situations beyond anyone's control. If the only thing you have to say is critical and negative, you are captive in a prison of your making. Gratitude facilitates forward motion. It allows you to look with hope toward tomorrow.

Gratitude Makes You More Aware of God's Love and Provision

So often, we pat ourselves on the back and brag about our accomplishments. But only those without vision think God is not alive, caring, gracious, merciful, and active in our world and our lives. Acknowledging God as creator, provider, and sustainer, and offering him your praise, results in wisdom, understanding, and greater blessings.

Just as the refining of precious metals takes time, refining your mindset toward blessings and gratitude is also a process, but one worth pursuing.

Does Gratitude Always Make Sense?

Is it reasonable to be thankful even when you are waiting and don't understand why? On the surface, no, but we can train ourselves to be grateful and praise God even when waves of adversity crash over us.

Looking back on difficult seasons in my life, I more readily understand the reasons to praise God even in challenging times. The Bible tells us to give thanks in all circumstances.

God is Our Hope

Praise is a catalyst for hope, propelling us mentally toward the time when waiting ends and a new season begins.

Job experienced heartache, adversity, acute physical pain and mental anguish, but despite all he endured he could still say of God, "Though he slay me, yet will I hope in him" (Job 13:15 KJV).

King David praised God with great enthusiasm, so much so, that his unabashed praise on the day he moved the Ark of the Covenant to Jerusalem embarrassed his wife.

While many of the psalms of David are cries for rescue from his enemies and protection, they also speak of God's promises and faithfulness. David valued his relationship with God so highly the reaction of others to his level of praise didn't matter to him.

David was an old man when he penned Psalm 71, which offers insight into the link between hope and praise. David knew from his long history with God that praise isn't contingent on circumstances. More praise enhances hope and bolsters faith in times of waiting. "But as for me, I will wait *and* hope continually, And will praise You yet more and more" (Psalm 71:14 AMP).

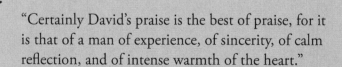

"Certainly David's praise is the best of praise, for it is that of a man of experience, of sincerity, of calm reflection, and of intense warmth of the heart."

~Charles H. Spurgeon,
The Treasury of David

We Have the Assurance of God's Love and Salvation

It is easy to succumb to discouragement when every plan is thwarted, every time frame shattered, control over situations is nonexistent, and waiting brings everything to a standstill. A synonym of discourage is dishearten, which means to lose hope, enthusiasm, or courage. Often, when you lose hope, it takes great effort to revive enthusiasm and raise spirits.

The psalmist David experienced many highs and lows in his lifetime, and his writings chronicle that ebb and flow. Some psalms are outright praise and thanksgiving. Others beg for rescue or detail injustice and discouragement. David's method for combating discouragement involved remembering God's miracles, meditating on God's mighty deeds, and verbalizing the faithful love of God and the gift of salvation.

Romans 8:38 (NIV) reminds us, no matter what we endure, "nothing can separate us from God's love." When you know Christ as Savior, your salvation and eternity are secure. This promise is balm for the soul when doubts, discouragement, and fears overwhelm.

Hardship Lasts Only for a Season

When waiting for answers or resolution to a situation or for God to act, it's difficult to imagine any improvement. Don't fall into the trap of thinking God doesn't care about you because he doesn't immediately answer prayers or change circumstances. God cares. He sees. He knows. And this season in your life will moderate.

To everything there is a season, A time for every purpose under heaven.

Ecclesiastes 3:1 NKJV

Being a Christian doesn't exempt us from challenge. In fact, Jesus told us we'd have trouble in this world. Yet we're often angry and surprised when we encounter hardships and times of waiting. Just remember, we have the ultimate victory because of Jesus' sacrifice on the cross. For this reason, we can praise God despite struggles.

Praise Isn't Contingent on Circumstances

Often, we associate praise with times of blessing. When we are thankful and joyful we offer praise, but what about when circumstances are unpleasant and life isn't going as we planned? Should we be expected to praise God in times of challenge?

The story of Hannah in Scripture is an example of praise in the midst of heartache. Hannah longed for a child, but could not conceive. In a time when producing offspring was the measure of a woman's worth, Hannah's barrenness was a source of suffering and emotional pain. To add to the difficulty of her situation, her husband's other wife, Peninnah, had children and delighted in taunting Hannah about her childlessness, especially each year when the family traveled to the temple to worship the Lord. Scripture says Peninnah enjoyed making Hannah feel miserable about not having children, reducing Hannah to tears and causing her to be so upset she could not eat.

Hannah had been waiting a long time for a child, and in that time of waiting, she also had to deal with the verbal abuse of someone in her household. It would have been understandable if Hannah had stayed at home when her family made the journey to the temple. For that brief span of time, she could escape the criticism and experience a measure of peace. Yet despite her heartache, she went to the temple and worshiped God. Even when the acid words of her rival were the most intense, Hannah still praised God.

Like Hannah, we can praise God even when our lives are in turmoil. We can praise God despite our circumstances.

Blessings

Blessings abound, but waiting produces tunnel vision, allowing focus only on the discomfort and uncertainty of current circumstances and clouding vision regarding the positive aspects of this season.

To successfully cope, as you wait, acknowledge all the ways you are blessed. Attune your mind and perception to small blessings each day, and the recognition of larger blessings throughout the waiting season. Small blessings may include the beauty of nature, the absence of physical pain, encouragement from an unexpected source, or an insight from Scripture that provides hope. Make a list, adding to it as you notice more evidence of God at work in your life. Each time you realize a blessing, praise God. As time goes by, you will see a pattern of blessings.

God's Character

God is worthy of praise regardless of our circumstances. We can praise him by remembering our position in relation to his holiness and power. In times of waiting, we learn to praise God for who he is instead of what he does. Consider God's attributes. He is faithful, compassionate, powerful, eternal, all-knowing, wise, infinite, unchanging, gracious, merciful, and loving. When you take time to reflect on who God is, praise becomes a natural overflow of the heart.

I will bless the Lord at all times; His praise will continually be in my mouth.

Psalm 34:1 KJV

Sacrificial Praise

*Therefore, let us offer through Jesus a continual
sacrifice of praise to God, proclaiming our allegiance to
his name.*

Hebrews 13:15 NLT

In Old Testament times, the law required daily sacrifices to God. The sacrifices and implementation of these sacrifices had to adhere to strict guidelines that were intricate, involved great attention to detail, and had to be carried out exactly as prescribed. Just reading the instructions is exhausting, so little wonder people grew weary with the directive to offer sacrifices and didn't always comply.

Today, we enjoy freedom from the daily rituals of sacrifices. Because of Jesus' death on the cross, his sacrifice for our sins, we are no longer bound by stringent rituals. Yet, praise is a sacrifice we can continually offer to God, minus restrictive guidelines. He is worthy of our praise.

Perhaps praise doesn't come easily for you, especially when circumstances in your life make praise a challenge. However, praise is a habit that can be cultivated. Begin with simple statements such as "I praise you, Creator God, for the beauty of nature" or "I praise you for providing wisdom in this decision."

Throughout the day, speak words of praise to God as you make observations and the Holy Spirit prompts. Enjoy praising God, knowing it is pleasing to him, a fragrant sacrifice.

*Make thankfulness your sacrifice to God and keep the
vows you made to the Most High.*

Psalm 50:14 NLT

Chapter 6

Exercising Faith in Waiting

But blessed is the one who trusts in the Lord, whose confidence is in Him. They will be like a tree planted by the water that sends out its roots by the stream. It does not fear when heat comes; its leaves are always green. It has no worries in a year of drought and never fails to bear fruit.

Jeremiah 17:7-8 NIV

A sturdy root system doesn't happen overnight. It takes time for roots to grow, spread, and find a life-sustaining water source. When rain is plentiful, plants can rely on groundwater for sustenance. But when drought comes, if a root system isn't deep enough to reach an underground water source, or stream, the plant may not survive.

Developing the type of trust that anchors in seasons of waiting, and other life struggles, is similar to a tree establishing a root system that supports, nourishes, and provides stability when wind and weather batter and toss.

Anchor

Years ago, the tallest tree in our backyard uprooted one night. It shook the ground and rattled the windows when it hit. To look at the tree, you'd never have guessed it was likely to fall. The trunk was massive and thick roots spread in all directions. Yet, after the tree fell, an inspection of the root end of the tree showed the entire root system was brittle and decayed, leaving the trunk hollow in the middle.

Our lives can be the same. To a casual observer, you may appear confident, successfully juggling all the balls in your world. You may even feel in control and secure in yourself, your abilities, and the support system you've established. But would you be able to handle an intense period of hardship or a period of waiting?

Many times, our root systems are damaged by lack of confidence, low self-esteem, negative self-talk, anger, or unforgiveness, creating a hollowness that is unseen by others, yet spills over into our thoughts and attitudes. Events or people may have contributed to the erosion. Perhaps you placed your trust in someone, only to be hurt when that person proved untrustworthy. Or maybe you experienced a pattern of betrayal that affects your willingness to risk trusting again. Examine your emotions regarding these incidents. Then take steps to grow healthier trust roots.

Surroundings

Often trees and plants spring up in places where they were not planted, awkward locations like a concrete expansion joint or beside the foundation of a building. These "volunteers" grow and flourish for a time, but eventually their surroundings cause them to be misshapen and stunted, making it impossible to sustain life.

While trees and plants can't choose their location, we choose where we go and with whom we associate. Initial involvement with people, organizations, or activities may feel rewarding, as if we are making headway, moving forward with goals, or advancing in a particular area. But not all advancement is conducive to growth.

Sometimes, too many thin roots running in multiple directions do nothing more than sap strength and thwart purpose. Choose carefully with whom you associate and where you focus involvement. Make sure you are receiving and growing rather than being sapped and diverted from what is best for you.

Nourishment

A root system does more than allow a tree or plant to remain upright. Roots are the pathway for water and nutrients. Sometimes, roots even help to prevent disease and encourage growth.

We usually think of nourishment only in terms of what we eat and drink. However, in order to remain healthy and strong as we weather waiting seasons, we also need mental, emotional, and spiritual nourishment. Many people discount these areas of nourishment and fail to feed themselves with continual learning, ways of expressing creativity, interaction with those who are grounded and wise, and the ingestion of spiritual food. But all are important to health, growth, and well-being.

Only by establishing and maintaining good relationships, continued learning, creative expression, and spiritual growth can we develop a strong root system that sustains when the storms of life come.

Developing trust is similar to maintaining a strong root system. If you haven't strengthened your trust roots by deeply embedding them in God's word, when seasons of waiting come, you may feel you are thirsty for reassurance and failing to bear fruit.

Embracing the P-words

In my seasons of waiting, I have found the following p-words helpful to remember—patience, protection, promise-keeper, and preparation.

Patience

It only takes a few minutes in traffic to be reminded that patience is not a quality most of us possess. Drivers blast horns the minute a light turns green, dart from lane to lane, squeeze in where there is not enough room, and endanger others simply to get beyond those they view as moving too slowly. Impatience is even more evident when someone has car trouble, or an accident slows the flow of traffic.

When my children were young, my car stopped in a busy intersection near the mall on a scorching summer day. Attempts to get the car moving again were fruitless, although I partially lowered the windows. Even with emergency flashers on, horns blared as people shot around us, gesturing and shouting. One man stopped beside us and let loose with a stream of profanity that left me in tears.

Patience is in short supply in our world. While remaining patient in traffic tests us on one level, exhibiting patience while in one of life's waiting rooms is even more challenging. However, if you learn to employ patience, treating it as an ally, a time of waiting will be more bearable. Waiting schools us in trust, but often the lessons are hard and require some tutoring. Only with repeated practice do we learn patience is synonymous with trust and learn to lean heavily on our Father.

Protection

> *Paul and his companions traveled throughout the region of Phrygia and Galatia, having been kept by the Holy Spirit from preaching the word in the province of Asia. When they came to the border of Mysia, they tried to enter Bithynia, but the Spirit of Jesus would not allow them.*

Acts 16:6-7 NIV

The chronicle of the apostle Paul's missionary journeys in the New Testament recounts several times when the Holy Spirit prevented Paul and his companions from entering certain regions. Paul was headstrong and could have ignored the directive to wait, but he paid attention to the prompting of the Holy Spirit and did not barrel ahead, ignoring the Spirit's message in favor of his plan.

Most of us have experienced occasions in air travel when the plane is in a holding pattern, circling the airport, waiting for the go-ahead from an air traffic controller to land. Especially if you have a tight connection for the next leg of the trip, hanging in midair, waiting for an invisible someone to allow moving forward is frustrating and annoying. Sometimes we forget the controller sees all the blips on the radar screen. He sees the potential danger involved in letting too many planes land too closely together. He factors in potential problems and decides based on a point of view we cannot access.

When God has you in a holding pattern, pay attention. Like an air traffic controller, he has a more global perspective and considers elements we cannot see. Recognize the directive to wait may be for your protection.

Overconfident Action

Most of us can probably remember a time when we ignored an internal prompting that warned not to move forward with plans or encouraged a different time frame. Moving forward despite God's directives often results in unpleasant consequences.

Many years ago, I was involved in developing acreage into lots. I was comfortable with the initial proposal, but then the land planner recommended the development of an additional section. Although I discussed it with the others involved, I ignored the internal voice that prompted waiting, and pushed for the expanded development. I felt confident the additional lots would sell because they were on a prime section of the property and I assumed would provide extra profit.

The addition to the project increased the time frame for completion, and during the process, the company building the roads pulled off our project to work on a more profitable endeavor. Months dragged by and potential buyers and builders lost interest and purchased in other areas. Loan payments came due, and the anticipated income from sales was not there to cover costs. Anxiety increased.

Six months after the project was finally completed, the bottom fell out of the real estate market, and we entered a long season of waiting for a turnaround. Although we made loan payments, they came at great personal sacrifice to those on the development team.

We all experience times when we hear from God and choose to ignore. It's human nature to resist being told what to do, but we forget God sees the whole scope of what lies ahead. He has watched the whole movie, while we have seen only the trailer or teaser.

Often, teasers are deceptive, conning us into believing something that isn't really going to happen. A snippet of one scene is spliced onto another, giving us a skewed perspective on reality. God not only sees the big picture, he wrote the script, and if we are wise, we allow him to direct.

Trust is the key. Trust almighty, omniscient, omnipresent God to instruct you in ways that provide for your protection while you wait for the next scene to unfold.

Promise-Keeper

The Lord always keeps his promises; he is gracious in all he does.

Psalm 145:13 NLT

Suppose you'd been on a four-decade journey. When the journey began, you were still a teen. In the ensuing years, you grew, learned, married, had children, became a grandparent; and all the while, you've been constantly on the move, hoping, waiting for the fulfillment of a promise. You grew weary, doubting whether the promise would actually be fulfilled. Perhaps you and the others misunderstood. Maybe disobedience negated the promise, or leaders failed to comprehend directives.

Suddenly, there are rumblings of an important assembly. Whispered information passes from person to person. Could this be it? Is this the long-expected announcement that ends forty years of waiting and wandering? The shofar sounds and hurried footfalls lead to a gathering. Bodies crowd together. Shhhh. Ears strain. Moses speaks.

When Moses gathered the Children of Israel, he gave them a history lesson. He reminded them who God is and what he'd done. Lest the full story be forgotten, Moses rolled verbal film on the previous forty years, and instructed the people to make sure successive generations never forgot what captivity was like as they entered a land of abundance.

Moses reminded the people that God went ahead of them on their journey. During the forty years, they lacked nothing—their clothes didn't wear out, and they had daily bread, meat, and everything they needed to survive.

God offers us the same provision, but often we're impatient. We usually try in our wisdom and timing rather than trusting God to provide while we wait for answers to prayer or a change of circumstances. Yet, when circumstances improve, and we move to a new season of life, we forget God is a faithful promise-keeper.

Deuteronomy reminds us to focus on God and trust him to fulfill his promises. Always keep in mind that God has proved a trustworthy promise-keeper for generation upon generation.

Preparation

As I watched a favorite epic film, *Out of Africa,* I was struck by all that must have gone into the preparation prior to beginning the filming: finding funding, selecting a scriptwriter, the writing, casting, gathering a crew, determining a filming location, making travel and housing arrangements, securing visas and permits, permissions, working with local hires, learning lines, making authentic period costumes, navigating weather, producing, filming, editing, distributing, and advertising. This list is only a portion of all that is involved in producing any sort of creative work, but the point is, in any endeavor, of epic proportions or not, extensive preparation is involved.

Preparation for seasons of waiting happens gradually. Each challenge, difficulty, or hardship that required you to acknowledge God and trust him for resolution was preparation for times of waiting.

Obedience is part of the trust equation. Any time you obey God instead of acting in your own strength and wisdom, and on your schedule, you strengthen your trust muscles. Those who have learned to trust God can rest confidently in waiting, believing God has their best interests in mind and will act on their behalf.

Trust–A Lifeboat in Stormy Seasons of Waiting

When everything goes according to our plans and expectations, trusting God is easy. But what happens when unexpected difficulties wash over your life in the same way an incoming tide surrounds, swirls, and crumbles an elaborate sandcastle you've spent all day building? How sturdy is your lifeboat when you're waiting out a storm?

Storm Clouds Brewing

One of my uncles was an air traffic controller and former pilot. Each year during our family beach vacations, he enjoyed sitting on the porch, watching the sea and sky. Once when dark clouds were rolling in and gusty wind whistled through the porch, I asked him why he was still outside. "I like to watch the weather," he said. "Over the years, I've learned to interpret the severity of storms."

Fishermen, farmers, and others who work outside know how to interpret the look of the sky to predict the weather. They know a red sky at night means good weather the next day, and a red sky in the morning means bad weather or a significant change in weather, is probably on the way.

Unlike storm watchers, we can't always tell when storms in our lives are about to arise or when we are about to plunge into a holding pattern. Sometimes, we can read the signs and know to expect what is ahead, but other times, something happens suddenly, everything changes, and it feels like our lives are falling apart.

Several difficult circumstances can happen at once. Rarely do we get to do one hard situation at a time. Jesus didn't promise a problem-free life. He said, "Here on earth you will have many trials and sorrows. But take heart, because I have overcome the world" (John 16:33 NLT). Trust is an anchor when waves of crisis crash over our heads.

Jesus First

When difficult circumstances bombard us, we often panic and grab for anything or anyone other than Jesus for help. Many times, Jesus is our last choice for explanation, comfort, and rescue.

Think about times when you've turned to other people for help in crisis situations or tried to push forward with your plans in seasons of waiting. Often our first response is to call or text a friend instead of praying. We talk about what is going on in our lives to anyone who will listen, spilling out our frustration over the unfairness of what has happened or the pointlessness of being forced into a waiting period.

People are full of advice, but it's often difficult to parse conflicting suggestions and determine if they are accurate or helpful for your situation. Then you're more confused than ever. Try turning to Jesus first. Pour out your confusion, frustration, and fears to him and patiently wait for him to answer. You may not hear an audible voice. Sometimes, his answers come quietly through the words of Scripture. That's why it's important to read God's word. Eventually, his answer may come to you in another way, but if you faithfully seek answers to life's problems in the pages of the Bible, and trust God in difficulties, and seasons of waiting, you will receive answers and comfort.

Avoid Superstition

People turn to superstitious beliefs rather than trust when life storms arise or seasons of waiting lengthen. Some believe events occur because of something they did or failed to do. Or they suspect they are being punished for not learning a certain lesson the first time and are now enduring hardship as a second learning opportunity.

Years ago, a woman asked a group I was a member of for prayer. She believed some area of sin in her life was the reason her relative was sick, that God was punishing her relative because the woman had unconfessed sin in her life. God doesn't work this way, and to believe he does is evidence of Satan twisting our thought processes. Yes, you may suffer personal consequences for your sin, but God doesn't give someone else cancer because you lied about something.

Give Thanks

When storm clouds rumble across your life, thankfulness is probably the last thing on your mind. We're more likely to complain or be mad at God for allowing chaos to interrupt the normal pattern of our days. But the Bible instructs us to find elements of thankfulness, even in difficulty. Often, this is extremely hard to do and requires us to trust that God is in control. Although we may not understand why, we can praise God for his great love for us in sending Jesus to die for our sins. We can thank him for the Holy Spirit, who walks beside us through the most difficult circumstances and helps us navigate times when we are forced to wait.

Pray

Many times, when we pray, it's all about telling, tattling, and begging, but not much about listening. We pray when we're in trouble, but have little time for interaction with God when everything is going smoothly. However, God wants us to stay in touch with him daily. That takes discipline because there are hundreds of distractions vying for our attention. It's easy to make excuses for why we don't have time to pray, but when you are already connected to God through a regular prayer life, it's much easier to handle crisis situations when they come. Having an intimate relationship with God through prayer provides peace and calmness.

Time Alone

Jesus realized the importance of spending time alone with God. The Bible mentions many times when he got up early, while his disciples were still sleeping, and withdrew to a place where he could be by himself and pray. He also pulled away from his followers after some of his greatest sermons and miracles. Perhaps he needed time to recharge physically and emotionally, or maybe he needed this time with his Father to refocus and realize anything he accomplished was because of God's power and provision.

We need time alone with God, too. When you stay busy all day and fall in bed exhausted at night, you miss important times of quietness and spiritual growth. Spiritual maturity prepares us for the storms of life and seasons of waiting.

Source of Security

Trust in Jesus Christ is like a lifeboat. Jesus plucks us out of stormy waters, places us in the lifeboat, wraps a warm, dry blanket around our shivering shoulders, and rows us to shore. When you accept Jesus as your savior, he invites you to step from the tossing waves into his lifeboat of eternal security and provides the strength and courage necessary to face daily challenges.

Hope

I wait for the Lord, my whole being waits, and in his word I put my hope.

Psalm 130:5 NIV

Trusting God to work out the details of what we're going through is probably one of the biggest challenges in the lives of Christians. By acknowledging God's control, we are better able to be at peace during times of waiting and trust God for next steps.

Hope is like a buoy that bobs us to the surface when waiting threatens to pull us under. Especially when waiting is prolonged, hope keeps us afloat.

Cindy's Story

When Cindy's husband received a cancer diagnosis, they embarked on a journey that involved tests, surgery, and waiting. They gained a fresh understanding of the power of prayer, and the necessity for trust as they entered a season of waiting.

"Wait seems to be the sign God keeps holding up in our faces. I have had to come to grips with that word … wait. In fact, I'm still working on it, but God has taught me wait means more than learning to stand still. It means looking for what is coming, not standing in one spot. It means fully understanding and trusting in His timing. And we all know, God's timing is never what we intend or expect.

"[Wait] means recognizing the value in slowing down, stepping gently over our hard moments rather than stomping impulsively through. I guess I'm learning there is more to waiting than I anticipated. It's really not God punishing us, but it's him saying, 'Oh, there is so much more. Hold up. You'll see.'

"Impatience nips at our heels. We just want this behind us. Still, as hard as the road is, the prince [her husband] and I are determined to seek this spiritual food. I say it once, I say it again. Faith grows trust. So, we seek to be faithful, to understand faith, to practice faith, and from that our trust simply becomes second nature.

"I am continually seeking the lessons learned from this side path God has us on, and so, Proverbs 3:5-6 came to mind. 'Trust in the Lord with all your heart and lean not on your own understanding; in all your ways submit to him, and he will make your paths straight.'

"Often, we look first to what we physically can see and touch rather than to the God who lives within us. Trust is hard sometimes, but I think God understands our weaknesses both tangible and intangible. He certainly prefers we learn to trust fully in Him, but in His loving faithfulness, He forgives our weakness and then gently nudges us toward learning trust.

"I'll be honest. Over these months of waiting, I've found my trust floundering just a tad. Despite my heart's desire to trust, fear made it seem so distant. God more than showed up on surgery day for Tim. But get this, [God] knew my weaknesses, my spots where I was missing trust, and He forgave that, then placed six people around me and my boys to stand in the gap. When my trust faltered, theirs rose like a WWW wrestler.

"I'm far from perfect, further from being everything God asks me to be, but no matter, God's faithfulness is immovable. Trust in the Lord. [I've learned] don't waste time on the tangible, and what I think is the way. Submit to Him and He will make your paths straight. Trust. Submit. Walk."

Chapter 7

Believing God's Faithfulness

Know therefore that the Lord your God is God, the faithful God who keeps covenant and steadfast love with those who love him and keep his commandments, to a thousand generations.

Deuteronomy 7:9 ESV

During the months following Jim's job loss, when we were without income, we saw God's provision in unexpected ways.

My father and Mr. Stephens, another real estate developer, opened a subdivision. A few lots remained when my father and Mr. Stephens died, and they eventually passed to me and Mr. Stephens' children. Over the years, the son who handled this property and I discussed ways to sell the remaining lots. But the lots were rough and crisscrossed with gullies.

After many years, an offer came for one lot, but it had contingencies, including an extended delay in closing of over a year. Because we really wanted to sell the property, we agreed to this unusual provision in the contract.

Personally, I expected the purchaser to default because the earnest money was insignificant and the time lapse until closing gave ample opportunity for the purchaser to reconsider. However, this purchaser owned adjoining property, so that was an incentive to follow through. I signed the contract, filed my copy, and promptly forgot about the upcoming transaction because the waiting period to closing was almost two calendar years away.

In January, after my husband lost his job in July, I got a call from Mr. Stephens' son. "Candy, can you close on that lot at the end of the week?" My mind swirled. Lot? Closing?

"You remember that lot we got a contract on 18 months ago? They're ready to close. Can you be at the attorney's office Friday at 3:00?"

The timing of that lot purchase, and the extended closing date that seemed so ridiculous when I signed the contract, suddenly made perfect sense in God's time frame. We had been trying to sell that lot for years, and when we finally got a contract, it had the quirky provision of an inordinate delay in closing. But with this sale came the financial provision we needed, at just the right time.

This experience taught me to trust and watch for God's creativity in providing for our needs, and reaffirmed God's faithfulness. You, also, can look for unique-to-you ways God is faithful in your time of waiting.

Lessons in Faithfulness

A family member battled cancer for years, with bone marrow transplants, massive doses of chemo, oral medication, and countless trips to the lab for blood analysis. For periods of time, he lived a normal life. At other times he was extremely ill and in great pain. Despite the wisdom of several doctors, the progression of cancer surpassed all medical treatment and stole precious years from his life. He, his family, and friends asked God to extend his life, and believed God could, but he died. The service in celebration of his life focused on Jesus, a testimony to his faithfulness to the Lord and the Lord's faithfulness to him and his family.

When Faith Challenges Come

Difficult situations like this challenge our faith. Sometimes, the person in crisis is not the one who doubts, but those around him. We choose our response to life situations, and those that don't seem to make sense to us require more insight. In anger and frustration, we can turn our backs on God, or choose to believe God's power and presence are available to help us through.

The biblical character Job faced such overwhelming issues his wife suggested he curse God and then die. Unwise advice, which Job did not accept. Job had experienced God's faithfulness in his lifetime and believed his situation would change or God would help him handle what was ahead.

Like Job, no one would have faulted my family member for cursing his situation, or God. Instead, he thanked God for His faithfulness and provision, remained strong in his faith, finished life well, and inspired others to live a life of faithfulness.

Committed, Focused, and Faithful

Often, we are committed to something when we first begin, like an exercise program, a Bible study, a training course, or pursuing an additional degree. But as time goes on, and distractions, disappointments, or delays come, we fall behind in what we planned to accomplish and eventually give up altogether.

Don't allow the challenges that result from a season of waiting to cause you to forget God's faithfulness. If you are struggling with evidence of God's faithfulness, take a mental inventory of times in the past when God has rescued, provided, sustained, and encouraged you. Satan wants you to question God's faithfulness, but experience will help you remember.

The apostle Paul's encouragement to Timothy to persevere and remain focused, not giving in to distraction or discouragement, is a reminder for us, too. Waiting may make you feel discouraged and hopeless, but faith carries you through.

But you must remain faithful to the things you have been taught. You know they are true, for you know you can trust those who taught you.

2 Timothy 3:14 NLT

Stockpiling Your Faith

During the time our country was expanding westward, settlers often marked their journey by traveling from one fortified outpost to another. If you've ever seen an old movie of the wild west, a fort conjures the image of sharp-pointed logs forming a fenced enclosure around a few buildings. Soldiers patrolled from an elevated platform, scanning the horizon for danger. Within the fort was a stockpile of ammunition, food, and water to provide support during attacks.

We need to stockpile our faith the way early fort-dwellers collected and stored supplies. One of the best ways to arm your faith is by reading God's word. A daily infusion of God's word is like getting a spiritual IV. Then, when challenging circumstances arise, seasons of waiting come, and Satan attacks you mentally, you have a firm grasp on Scripture to provide wisdom, direction, and peace.

Relying on Faith

My father was in the U.S. Army Air Corps during World War II. After training stateside, he was stationed in Algiers and Tunisia, flying bombing missions over Germany. Each mission was fraught with tension, anxiety, and uncertainty. Each mission might be the last for someone, or for the whole crew and had the potential result of capture or death.

Back home, his parents had several sons serving in the war. One day, my grandfather came home from his lumberyard and noticed my grandmother had circled a date on the calendar with a red pen. When he questioned her about the date, she said, "I don't know why I circled that date, but the Lord told me to circle it and pray."

"I circled that same date today on the calendar in my office," said my grandfather.

Realizing they had received a message from God, they prayed and waited. Finally, word came that my father's plane had been shot down. The date my father was listed as missing in action was the date my grandparents had circled on their calendars. Now they knew God had been preparing them for this waiting season.

As the parents of nine children and having lost their home and business during the Great Depression, they had experienced God's faithfulness firsthand and trusted that no matter what the outcome, that faithfulness would endure.

Eventually, word came that my father was alive, but had been captured and was an internee in Switzerland. Contact was limited, and for long periods of time there was no information about his condition.

When my father's plane was shot down and he bailed out, he didn't know what country he was in. He and his comrades walked until they came to a border, but they didn't know which side was which country. They crossed over and were captured by a Swiss patrol. Did the faithful prayers of my grandparents aid in the decision to cross the border? I believe they did.

After prolonged captivity, my father escaped through the Underground, a resistance movement.

That season of waiting for my grandparents, and my father, would have been unbearable without their knowledge and reliance on the faithfulness of God.

Seek Encouragement

When we experience difficult situations and times of waiting, any form of encouragement provides hope. For my grandparents, hope came in occasional correspondence from their son and the knowledge that many were praying for his safe return and for them.

There are ways to receive encouragement as you wait.

- Be aware you are not the only person who has encountered challenging circumstances or waiting periods. Others have walked rugged paths before you and made it through. Realize you were not singled out for some sort of punishment, because that's not true.
- Look at the lives of those who have faced challenges, responded in a positive manner, and remained strong in their faith. Let them be your role models.
- Rest in the assurance that others are praying for you and are concerned about you. Draw strength from that knowledge.

- Tell God aloud you believe he is faithful and you trust him. Sometimes, just affirming your faith out loud gives you courage.
- Daily look for evidence of God's love and faithfulness. "Because of the Lord's great love we are not consumed, for his compassions never fail. They are new every morning; great is your faithfulness" (Lamentations 3:22-23 NIV).

Be Faithful in Prayer and Worship

When life is difficult, we often bail out on prayer and worshiping with a body of believers. Perhaps we withdraw because we're mad at God, but stopping conversations with God is like starving yourself. Continue praying. Tell God exactly what you are thinking and feeling, even if you're angry. God won't punish you for honestly stating what you feel. But don't forget to listen also. God may speak to you through a sermon, a teacher, someone you hardly know, the words of a praise song, or directly to you in a quiet moment. Be open and receptive instead of closing yourself off. Even if you feel far from God, he speaks in a way that penetrates your distance and animosity.

Remember God's Faithfulness

Sometimes, when we face difficult circumstances associated with waiting, it feels like God has abandoned us. Satan wants us to think that, but God is faithful, merciful, and loving. Often, challenges and seasons of waiting are the catalyst for spiritual growth. So, while it may seem like God doesn't care what you're going through, he does. He understands the struggles we face and walks with us through them. Later, we can look back and see that he even carried us. We can also see how our faith has grown, but only if we allow difficulties to be a means of spiritual development rather than giving up on our faith because we've experienced something hard.

Faithfulness Has Rewards

When you begin some type of physical conditioning, it often takes a long time to see results. Weightlifters may not see muscle definition for weeks. Those attempting to lose weight often reach a plateau after an initial weight loss and are stuck there for a long time. That's when most people give up. They aren't willing to wait for the reward that will eventually come if they persevere.

Proverbs 3:3-4 reminds us, "Let love and faithfulness never leave you; bind them around your neck, write them on the tablet of your heart. Then you will win favor and a good name in the sight of God and man."

Remaining faithful takes work, but over time, it is worth the effort to finish strong. In the words of the apostle Paul, "I have fought the good fight, I have finished the race, and I have remained faithful. And now the prize awaits me—the crown of righteousness, which the Lord, the righteous Judge, will give me on the day of his return. And the prize is not just for me but for all who eagerly look forward to his appearing" (2 Timothy 4:7-8 NLT).

Look beyond current hardship toward the finish line and faithfully run the race before you, even if that race sidelines you in a period of waiting.

Chapter 8

Quieting Satan's Voice

*Be careful—watch out for attacks from Satan, your
great enemy. He prowls around like a hungry, roaring
lion, looking for some victim to tear apart. Stand
firm when he attacks. Trust the Lord; and remember
that other Christians all around the world are going
through these sufferings too.*

1 Peter 5:8-9 TLB

A pair of hawks frequent our backyard. Edged with lush
vegetation, tall trees, and a drainage stream, our yard is the
perfect location for the hawks to search for unsuspecting prey.
The birds situate themselves on high branches on opposite sides
of the yard, watching and waiting. At intervals, they call to each

other, reporting their findings. Sometimes, one flies to a branch closer to the other following a call out. They speak to each other, perhaps planning the best strategy for their impending conquest. Then, with practiced precision, they swoop down, one and then the other, grab their prey in sharp talons, and fly to a secluded location to feast.

One day, as I watched the hawks, I thought of our enemy, Satan, and how he observes us, watching for an unguarded moment to pounce an area of weakness, uncertainty, or doubt, and pick it apart. During life pauses, we are especially susceptible to attacks from the Enemy.

Satan, the Hijacker

The word "hijack" conjures scenes of gunmen commandeering an aircraft, or some other form of transportation, and making demands for money, or something else beneficial to the hijackers. The climate of a hijacking is always tense, replete with threats, fear, and dread. Sometimes captors decide to fight back.

Let's Roll chronicles the story of Todd Beamer, who was aboard United Airlines Flight 93 when it was hijacked as part of the September 11th terrorists' attacks in 2001. Seated near the back of the plane, Todd carried on a conversation with a GTE Airfone customer service representative for 13 minutes before he and several other passengers rushed the hijackers.

No one survived the crash of flight 93, but Beamer's recorded conversation provides evidence that passengers tried to thwart the hijackers' plans. Although they lost their lives, they prevented the hijackers from hitting their intended target, which was surely not a field in rural Pennsylvania.

In seasons of waiting, Satan hijacks our thoughts in a way similar to the gunmen who took over planes on September 11, 2001.

Often, we're unaware our thoughts are about to be hijacked as were those seated next to the hijackers before the takeover. Satan is cunning, and his words seem like rational thoughts. Sly phrases drip from his lips, stirring up doubts and planting fears. His persistent lies enhance the anxiety of waiting and cause us to doubt God's power and ability to act in our best interests.

Overcoming Doubt

Many times, hesitating and doubting the authenticity of what we've been told saves us from making life-changing mistakes. Sometimes courage is required to doubt because it's a lot easier to just accept what others say as truth rather than asking questions or delaying a decision.

However, is it ever okay to doubt God? Should we question why we are parked in a waiting zone when it makes perfect sense to us for everything to fall into place and our plans to happen now?

Scripture paints a picture of doubt in the disciple Thomas. After Jesus' resurrection, he appeared to some of his disciples, but Thomas was not with them. When they reported they had seen Jesus, Thomas wasn't willing to take their word that Jesus was alive. He said he wouldn't believe unless he could see the nail prints in Jesus' hands and touch the place in his side where the spear pierced him.

When Jesus appeared to the disciples again, Thomas was still reluctant to believe. Perhaps Thomas doubted because Jesus' appearance was altered in its resurrected form. Yet Jesus didn't chastise Thomas for his doubt. He simply showed Thomas his hands, and his side, and encouraged Thomas to touch the wounds to further verify their authenticity. Jesus provided the tangible evidence Thomas needed to believe.

Maybe, like Thomas, you are a doubter. Don't feel guilty, or ashamed, or measure your faith against that of others. Just confess your doubt and ask God for the evidence you need to believe. Then trust him.

We wouldn't be human if we didn't doubt. But doubting God's love and faithfulness in seasons of waiting can cripple us and provide an opportunity for Satan to gain a foothold, consuming our thoughts and distorting truth.

Confront Fears

Fear is an emotion we all face. But if we allow it, fear can dominate our lives and cause us to delay decisions. How is fear linked to doubt? Fear says, "don't take the risk." In times of waiting, don't take the risk translates into don't trust God, because you might be disappointed. Evaluate how fear is related to your doubts. Then, ask God to help you determine whether your fear is realistic for the situation and to remind you of his faithfulness.

Factor in Past Experiences

If you've ever been the subject of gossip, the victim of a liar, or disappointed by someone, you may be more inclined to doubt. Prior bad experiences make us hesitant because we don't want to risk being hurt or made to feel foolish again.

Often, we blame God for challenging circumstances in our lives, when, in fact, we sometimes have a hand in creating them. Take an honest look at your history with God and you will see he proves trustworthy over and over. While people will let you down, God never will.

Recognize the Evil One

Satan is more than a character in a red suit with a pitchfork tail. He is a subtle deceiver who loves to plant little seeds of doubt in our minds and water them with accusations cleverly cloaked as truth. Satan whispers, "If God really loved you, he wouldn't allow you to go through something this painful. He wouldn't place you in a waiting room and leave you there indefinitely without explanations."

Satan is the father of all lies. When he causes us to doubt God's love for us, Satan is overjoyed. He has been sowing seeds of doubt since the Garden of Eden, when he suggested God's reason for telling Adam and Eve not to eat from the tree of knowledge was for a purpose other than their protection.

Adam and Eve trusted Satan instead of relying on what they knew to be true about God. They moved forward without consulting God, making a decision that altered the course of their lives and the lives of all who came after.

Combating Doubt

Even those who are spiritually strong, and sure of God's purpose for their lives, are susceptible to doubt.

John the Baptist was Jesus' forerunner, the one who prepared the way, telling the people the arrival of the Messiah was imminent. John spoke confidently and with assurance that Jesus was the long-awaited Redeemer. Yet, as John sat in Herod Antipas's prison, awaiting execution, he was riddled with doubt.

Although prophets were never popular, and were often imprisoned or killed for prophecies leaders viewed as negative or threatening, John suddenly doubted that the one he proclaimed was indeed the Messiah.

Don't miss the fact that John was waiting, and the end of that waiting period was not relief but a gruesome death. Perhaps John expected Jesus to rescue him, and when that did not happen, doubt took over. As John waited in an uncomfortable, inescapable, fearful situation, he sent two of his followers to ask

Jesus, "Are you the Messiah we've been expecting, or should we keep looking for someone else?" (Luke 7:19 NLT)

Often, when we are waiting, doubt produces a similar level of uncertainty and fear. What we once were very sure of suddenly feels like we've been on the wrong track. Overcoming those doubts requires action.

Focus on Bible Promises

The only way you can know what God promises is to spend time in his word. Proverbs 2 promises that if we store God's commandments within, we'll gain knowledge, wisdom, and understanding. These allow us to make wise decisions without being overwhelmed by doubts. God's word anchors us and enhances patience during periods of waiting.

Believe God Wants the Best for You

Sometimes it feels like God doesn't care about us at all. During difficult situations and times of unexplained waiting, it's normal to doubt God's love and compassion, thinking he is unaware of our circumstances and our anguish. But God always has our best interests in mind. Genesis 50:20 reminds us that what others intend to harm us, God can use to our benefit. And Jeremiah 29:11 says God has a plan for our lives that prospers us, provides hope, and assures a future.

Strengthen your Faith

Athletes don't suddenly decide to compete in the Olympics. Years of training and physical development are required before an athlete is qualified for Olympic-level competition. Just as it requires time and training to build muscles, put some effort into building your faith. If you don't exercise faith regularly, your trust in God will remain weak and ineffective, allowing doubts to take center stage in your life.

James 1:6 equates asking God and then doubting him to waves of the sea, tossed one way and then another. By trusting God's faithfulness to see our circumstances, know our needs, and answer our prayers, we strengthen our faith. God proved himself faithful in many situations and to many people. His faithfulness didn't just happen in Bible times. It still happens today.

Resist Satan's Lies

Satan is real and enjoys speaking lies, but we don't have to believe those lies. We can tune out Satan's voice by refusing to allow ourselves to fall into patterns of doubt and negative thoughts. James 4:7 reminds us to "Resist the devil, and he will flee." Any time we resist Satan's lies that cause us to question God, we take a step forward in overcoming doubt.

Additional Weapons in Satan's Arsenal

If Satan can't plague you with doubts, he'll employ two additional powerful weapons—discouragement and fear. John 10:10 reminds us Satan seeks "to steal, and to kill, and to destroy." Most people view John's warning as a personal attack, stealing possessions, inflicting bodily injury, or ending life. Instead, perhaps it refers to stealing your faith, killing your trust, and destroying your hope.

Utilize the Power of Scripture to Recognize and Combat Satan

Have you ever encountered someone who plays devil's advocate? Such a person asserts an adversarial opinion to stir up debate or test the strength of opposing arguments. I have known several devil's advocates, and being around them was exhausting because even a casual comment was considered an invitation to counter with an opposing opinion, question what you said, and attempt to start a debate.

Satan, the devil himself, is skilled at baiting and taunting us into questioning what we know is true. He capitalizes on periods of waiting, physical discomfort, fatigue, and emotional upheaval, pouncing when we are most vulnerable. He taunts with if-then scenarios designed to make us question God's laws and promises.

Jesus spent forty days alone with Satan in a remote location. Each time Satan offered a way out of his discomfort, Jesus responded by quoting Scripture. If Jesus hadn't memorized Scripture or spent time daily with his father in prayer, he would have been much less equipped to resist the tempting options Satan offered. He relied on what he knew to be truth, and had committed to memory, instead of arguing. Not only does Scripture remind us of truth, but it is also an effective weapon against the mind-games Satan uses to cause us to doubt our faith.

Scripture is powerful. It reminds us of God's promises and covenants, which warn, provide encouragement, and help us make wise decisions. The stories in Scripture are those of everyday happenings and situations that still occur today to ordinary people, just as they did long ago. We face similar trials and tests. Scripture provides insights for resisting Satan's tricks. Quoting or reading Scripture turns the volume down on Satan's voice. Satan cannot refute Scripture because he knows it is truth.

Voice Recognition

When I was a child, finding a station on a transistor radio was sometimes difficult. While you knew the general location of the station on the dial, zeroing in on a clear voice required slowly turning the knob to weed out static and bleed-over from other stations. Even then, you depended on recognizing the announcer's voice to determine if you were really on the right station.

Learning to distinguish between God's voice and Satan's is sometimes a challenge. Satan is cunning, and like a con artist, knows how to "throw" his voice so it sounds as if it's coming from God. Ultimately, Satan is a shouter, while God speaks with a quiet, internal voice. When you are waiting, Satan's voice is often louder, drowning out the voice within. Sometimes, the voices of others add to the clamor. While you know God is there, your mind plays tricks on you, causing you to believe the lies of the loudmouth.

In conversation with a young man who attempted to take his life, he characterized his struggle with choosing life or death as one in which he felt he had an angel on one shoulder and the devil on the other. He heard "don't do it" from one voice and "do it" from the other. Eventually, the "do it" advice from Satan's voice became louder and stronger, and the young man plunged to what he assumed would be his death. Thankfully, although severely injured, his life was spared.

During life pauses, God is where he's always been, and who he always is. God is unchanging, eternal, faithful. His promises are true, and his love and concern for the difficulties in our lives are constant. Any voices you hear that are not in line with the truths of God's word and his character are not worthy of your attention.

No matter how often or loudly Satan tells you differently, in waiting, and every season of life, God is faithful.

Chapter 9

Facing Emotions While Waiting

It is the Lord who goes before you. He will be with you; he will not leave you or forsake you. Do not fear or be dismayed.

Deuteronomy 31:8 ESV

Suppose you were told you are about to be freed from years of slavery and oppression. Initially, you are skeptical because all you've known are cruel taskmasters and unrelenting labor. But despite skepticism, at some point, a tiny trickle of hope bubbles up.

You are instructed to be ready to travel, and finally, after great commotion, pestilence, and plagues, the day arrives to leave. The bubble of hope, that had almost vanished, turns into a rushing brook of joy as you move from a place of despair toward a place of promise. You sing with family members and friends as you march across the desert.

But soon, murmurs stir. Someone rushes forward from the back of the line, shouting, but you can't quite make out his words. Those around you look back, and suddenly, the words of another runner become clear as you realize an army is chasing you. The captors, who gave permission for you to leave, are now pursuing, intent on killing, or forcing you back into a life of slavery. Fear overwhelms as realization dawns that the only escape route is a sea too vast to cross.

People panic. Chaos ensues.

Then, your leader raises his arms and instructs you to be brave, stand firm, be still, to wait and watch as God rescues by fighting the battle for you.

Emotion Commotion

The Children of Israel are our go-to group for emotions experienced while waiting. At least five generations had waited 400 years for freedom from captivity, so it's no wonder they were afraid and skeptical that freedom was possible. When slavery is all you've known, the concept of anything different is hard to imagine. Even after breaking free from the Egyptians, their waiting wasn't over. Although they didn't know it when they crossed the Red Sea, their wait to reach the Promised Land would involve another 40 years.

Sometimes, waiting feels like someone pushed the pause button on your life. But while waiting may force us to slow down, we are often the ones who put ourselves in suspended animation, a state in which we don't feel or experience. However, if you allow it, the slowdown forces you to examine emotions, and that's something most of us avoid.

Inherent in waiting are anxiety, frustration, fear, anger, and defeat, indifference, and boredom. Never has that become more apparent than during these unsettled times. Unrest, riots, looting, political bantering, and the uncertainties inherent in a world-wide pandemic precipitate a wide spectrum of emotions that play out in numerous forms. While some respond to difficulties with calmness, multiple changes and waiting for what comes next bring out the worst in others.

During seasons of waiting, take time to examine and process what you are feeling. How do you accomplish this? For some, journaling allows for the release and examination of emotions. For ›others, talking about what they are experiencing is a more effective approach. With either method, you move from pause to slow-motion and eventually gain enough speed to move forward.

A caution: resist the urge to dump your emotions on social media.

I see social media posts that run the gamut from overt cries for sympathy to berating friends for not caring enough. Sometimes responders claim their lives are worse.

While you may initially get encouraging comments when you express emotions on social media, you also open yourself up to those who always respond with criticism and hatred, no matter what the post. The negativism, criticism, and hatred expressed by others, even strangers, creates additional tension and frustration that make you feel even worse.

Instead, pray about the emotions you are experiencing as you wait and allow God to speak to you. This spiritual interaction will benefit you in ways virtual commentary never could.

Fear

When my grandson was crawling and learning to walk, he was fearless. He thought nothing of crawling into another room, leaving my sight, and exploring well beyond my reach. When he began walking, it was the same. But several months before his second birthday, he was fearful of going into another room without me, especially if he heard a noise he couldn't identify, like the ice maker making more ice, the click of the thermostat, or an unidentifiable noise outside.

Fear often grows more intense as we age, perhaps because we have had more fear-producing life experiences.

My father was in his early twenties when he served in World War II. During one bombing mission, the bomb bay doors failed to open all the way and the bombs would not release. In a daring maneuver, Daddy walked the narrow catwalk between the partially opened doors and manually dropped the bombs. When he told that story, I asked him if he feared falling. A lopsided grin lifted the corner of his mouth and he said, "No, I had no fear. When you're twenty, you think you can do anything."

We experience something similar when life is on hold. We are fearless when our world is moving smoothly and we don't have any great cause for concern, but when we're forced into a waiting period, fear makes an appearance. When fear arrives, it drags a few friends along—anxiety and doubt. Satan uses the fear-anxiety-doubt trifecta as a powerful weapon to cause us to question our circumstances and God.

While we sometimes equate fear with tears, for some people fear prompts the emotion of anger. Often, that anger is misdirected at someone other than the source. For example, a person who loses his job and is in a period of limbo while waiting for employment may berate a server in a restaurant or customer service personnel in a store, instead of expressing anger toward the person who dismissed him from his job.

Fear is an emotion that feeds off itself. The more you focus on your fears, the more they take control of your mind. When our daughter was in elementary school, she had a friend who was terrified of tornadoes. Although the child had not experienced a tornado, she had watched the movie *Twister* repeatedly. The parents did not limit her exposure to this movie or calm her fears. On a school trip, the child panicked when the sky darkened, and a thunderstorm approached, because she equated the look of the sky with what she had seen on the movie. Feeding fears, instead of quelling them, enhances the power for fear to take control.

Sometimes, fear prompts action, but when action is not coupled with thought and responsibility, activity born of fear may lead to detrimental consequences. When we take action based on feelings and emotions instead of trusting God, we thwart what God is doing or about to do.

Fear can also shackle, holding you captive in a cycle of what-if scenarios and preventing growth that moves you forward when God opens a way of transition from waiting.

Anxiety

During the Vietnam War, Colonel Ted Ballard was imprisoned for years in the infamous "Hanoi Hilton." Much of that time, he was in solitary confinement, a method used to isolate prisoners, so they don't receive encouragement and support from each other.

During those years, the anxiety of waiting for what might happen next was overwhelming. Waiting involved wondering who would be chosen next for interrogation and torture, if food would be provided, if death were imminent, and far on the periphery, if rescue would ever come.

Amid their impossible situation, the prisoners communicated. They tapped messages in Morse Code that included The Lord's Prayer and passages of Scripture they could remember. One prisoner used scraps to make an American flag, which he kept hidden, except for times when the prisoners recited the Pledge of Allegiance and sang the national anthem.

Eventually, their North Vietnamese captors destroyed the flag and beat the man who made it. His fellow prisoners tended his wounds, and that night he again began piecing together another American flag.

Hope was a crucial part of the prisoners' ability to survive.

> *We wait in hope for the Lord; he is our help and our shield. In him our hearts rejoice, for we trust in his holy name. May your unfailing love be with us, Lord, even as we put our hope in you.*

Psalm 33:20-22 NIV

While my situation does not compare with Colonel Ballard's, I experienced anxiety in a way I never had before as I prepared to sell my childhood home. My father built the house in 1951, and my parents lived there until their deaths. The house was full of memories and the remnants of their lives and mine.

Following my mother's death, our son and his family lived in the house. The night he and his wife told us they had put a contract on a house in another town, I had what I assume was a panic attack. I had never experienced anything similar, and it took a while for me to sort my emotions.

Some of my anxiety was related to no longer having these loved ones in town. Some was tied to having to sift through the remaining items inside the house and in a carport storage room, items too difficult to process years ago, but now unavoidable. Eventually, I identified the real source of my anxiety was preparing to place the house on the market for sale and saying goodbye to a place that was synonymous with love, happiness, and security.

A change in the familiar is often at the heart of anxiety. Waiting changes the normal rhythms of life, causing us to let go of the familiar cadence of our days and make adjustments that render the normal flow choppy.

While I had anxiety about selling my family home, I also experienced anxiety regarding scheduling contractors to make repairs and spruce up the property, along with the wait involved in having them complete the tasks. Once the house went on the market, my anxiety shifted to how many showings were scheduled and the comments following the showings. Even after a receiving a contract, I allowed anxiety about the inspection process to rob me of peace.

I'd like to say I handled the anxiety well. I did not. Sleepless nights, digestive issues, and anger were all part of my anxiety experience. Issues unrelated to selling the house also seemed to be magnified.

As you wait, get help when anxiety overwhelms. It's not a sign of weakness to admit a struggle with anxiety and take steps to combat it.

Uncertainty

The uncertainty of waiting brings an uneasiness that many of us do not handle well. We enjoy the reliability of routine, and it's disconcerting when circumstances beyond our control alter the familiar. Often, we are resistant when God instructs to wait. Human nature wants to call the shots, and it takes self-control and patience to willingly accept and navigate a time of waiting.

Anger

COVID changed our way of life. To slow the spread of the virus and minimize the death toll, state mandates closed businesses, transitioned school to home learning, and shuttered churches. The resulting panic produced shortages, tanked the stock market, furloughed workers, and quarantined families in their homes. As we entered a season of watching and waiting, fears increased, even as many bristled at restrictions that altered day-to-day life and created stress and financial strain.

After weeks of stay-at-home orders and closed businesses, people pushed back against restrictions, opening businesses ahead of time, and protesting with violent demonstrations and criminal activity.

In a waiting period, anger usually emerges, overshadowing reason and perpetrating violent actions and reactions. Anger can come in many forms and be directed at numerous targets. Unfortunately, angry arrows often find a home in the hearts of those we claim to love the most.

And then, there is anger directed toward God. God is a convenient target. He is invisible and doesn't engage in verbal banter. It is not unusual for people to choose God as the recipient of their anger in a time of waiting because they blame him for current circumstances rather than shouldering any responsibility themselves. While God is big enough to take your anger, distancing yourself from God in anger during a season of waiting is like cutting the rope on a life preserver thrown to you while drowning. God is your best resource and advocate in waiting, so work through anger, and reach for his help.

God created all emotions. They serve as an expression of exuberant celebration, and also, as an outlet for stress, but Scripture cautions that emotions should be held in check, controlled, and not allowed to take over. While it may take great effort, work toward balancing emotions, and refuse to allow fear, anxiety, uncertainty, and anger to take control and prevent you from learning and growing while you wait.

Life's Waiting Rooms

Early in the COVID-19 pandemic, I accompanied my 94-year-old aunt to a lab appointment. I had been with her before, and as she signed in at the window, I walked toward a seat in the empty waiting room. I had barely touched down on the chair before the receptionist leaned out the window separating her desk from the lobby and announced, "I'm sorry, but you can't be here. You must leave." She explained that because of the pandemic, the waiting area must remain unoccupied. "Please wait in your car, and we will bring your aunt to you when her lab work is done."

Waiting rooms are often some of the most miserable places imaginable. Whether waiting for your appointment, procedure, or surgery, or that of a loved one, waiting rooms are synonymous with anxiety, stress, fear, and confinement.

Many years ago, my father-in-law was in a critical care unit following a heart attack. I still remember the long hours spent in the waiting area between limited visiting hours. The hospital was only 30 minutes from my in-laws' home, but the schedule for visiting hours was such that going to their house was not practical. While we were free to leave the waiting area, going somewhere in the car involved the daunting task of finding a place to park when we returned.

Although we could walk within the hospital or on the grounds, we were hesitant to be out of reach (this was before cell phones) too long given the seriousness of my father-in-law's condition. So, we spent long days in the waiting room, praying for improvement that would allow transitioning to a different type of waiting.

People handle waiting room stays in various ways. Some attempt to sleep on uncomfortable chairs with intrusive armrests.

129

Others talk, incessantly, to those with them, on cell phones, or to unsuspecting strangers with no hope of escape. People stare, retreating to a different place mentally. Still others are restless, pacing, or finding any excuse to leave and return.

Years later, when the receptionist asked me to leave the waiting room, I pondered how often I've wished someone would dismiss me from one of life's waiting rooms. I remember the emotions, stress, discomfort, and fatigue of waiting with no means of calculating the length of the wait or determining the outcome. One variable of waiting involves not knowing if you can base a current time of waiting on a previous waiting experience. Occasionally, mercifully, waiting ends sooner than you expect.

You are Excused

While some people enjoy jury duty, I do not. In my mind, a jury summons is synonymous with a week of long waits and lost freedom. I had been dreading my civic duty for over a month when the day came to report to the courthouse.

I arrived that Monday morning with a thick book, determined to make the most of the inevitable slow wheels of justice that equal extended periods of waiting while nothing happens. The initial roll call was followed by a lengthy span of—you guessed it—waiting. I plowed through the first few chapters of my book before the clerk of court appeared. She was smiling. I'd never seen a clerk of court look even remotely happy, let alone smile, so what did this mean?

"Thank you for showing up today," she said, her smile broadening. "Many jurors ignore a jury summons. One of our judges dislikes that so much he sends officers to pick up jurors who don't show up. You, however, are going to be rewarded for the decision you made to come today. These names you see on the board are those who made a different decision and they will not be rewarded. In fact, they will be thrown back into the jury pool. You, however, are going to experience something unusual. This rarely happens, but the cases on the docket for this session, all of the cases, have been resolved and you are excused for the week. You are free to go."

A momentary, stunned silence blanketed the room, followed by an eruption of cheers and applause. As we filed out of the building, en masse, crossed the street, and headed toward the parking garage, the woman beside me said, "Right now, we are the happiest people in town!"

Happiness is often elusive when waiting, but we can take joy in the knowledge of pardoned sin through Jesus' sacrifice on the cross and the reward of heaven that awaits. No matter what season of life we are experiencing, our enthusiasm should equal, or exceed, that of excused jurors as we recognize the magnitude of God's grace and provision in our lives. We serve a powerful, loving, merciful, and forgiving God. Rejoice in that knowledge and trust him for what lies ahead.

There is no other God like you! You forgive sin and pardon the rebellion of those who remain among your people. You do not remain angry forever, but delight in showing loyal love.

Micah 7:18 NET

Chapter 10

Moving Forward While You Wait

The Lord Almighty, the God of Israel sends this message to all the captives he has exiled to Babylon from Jerusalem: Build homes and plan to stay; plant vineyards for you will be there many years. Marry and have children, and then find mates for them and have many grandchildren. Multiply! Don't dwindle away! The truth is this: You will be in Babylon for seventy years. But then I will come and do for you all the good things I have promised and bring you home again. For I know the plans I have for you, says the Lord. They are plans for good and not for evil, to give you a future and a hope.

Jeremiah 29: 4-6, 9-11 TLB

Often, a season of waiting feels like exile, captivity, even abandonment. Perhaps, like the Babylonian captives, you are so focused on what feels like imprisonment, you've become immobile in your season of waiting. No one wants to think a period of waiting is going to stretch on for months or seventy years, but we can learn important lessons from Jeremiah's words to the Babylonian exiles.

God sent a message through the prophet Jeremiah to the people of Israel, giving them instructions on what to do while in captivity. He told them the length of their wait and what to do while they waited. He instructed them to build houses, find mates, have children and grandchildren, work, and prosper. In essence, God instructed the people to get on with their lives and enjoy living where they were and in the circumstances in which they found themselves.

The words "don't dwindle away" are especially powerful. Sometimes, when we are in a season of waiting, we allow our circumstances, our disappointment, discouragement, and frustration with the situation to send us into a tailspin. We spiral downward emotionally and fail to benefit from a time of waiting. But there are lessons to be learned in waiting, and those lessons prepare us for what comes next. During periods of waiting, you don't have to sit idly by. You can prepare to move forward when the waiting is over.

Waiting Rooms

Over the years, I've spent more time than I've wanted to in waiting rooms, literally and figuratively. I've endured long anxious hours in hospital waiting rooms or the emergency department of our local hospital, as well as complicated emotional waiting seasons, praying for resolutions to situations, answers, change, or confirmation.

Regardless of the type of waiting you're currently experiencing, moving forward as you wait is a tricky endeavor because waiting is often paralytic. Waiting feels like stagnation, but it's possible to move forward in other areas of life while you wait in another.

While the ER is never a place most of us would choose to visit, we can learn from the experience. As I spent a night in the ER, I made some observations.

The Unexpected Happens

No matter how careful we are, we are not always in control. When I was learning to drive, my father always said, "You've got to watch out for the other fellow." I understood this to mean being careful involved steering clear of someone else's carelessness. Sometimes injury results from no fault of your own. Other times, you make a misstep and find yourself somewhere you didn't expect to be. Illness or injury crop up when you least expect them, and usually, at inopportune times. The same is true of seasons of waiting. You can bemoan the situation, or you can adjust, adapt, and move forward where possible. The choice is yours.

Waiting is a Given

One of the most difficult parts of a visit to the ER is the wait involved. You know before you arrive that you can expect a prolonged experience, yet are always hopeful this time it will be speedier. Life rarely happens on our timetable. No one enjoys waiting, but sometimes it's to your benefit. You may have a more positive outcome or see the resolution of a problem if you wait instead of pushing for something to happen. God often allows a waiting room sojourn to teach or protect. His plan is always better for you than an outcome you manufacture on your own.

Patience is Required

In any area of life, practicing patience is probably one of the most challenging qualities to master. The world conditions us to expect instant everything, so patience must be cultivated. Often impatience and anger are conjoined twins, overlapping and intertwined. Investigating the roots of impatience is the first step toward perfecting the art of patience.

Trust is Necessary

When you make yourself available to emergent care, you place your trust in someone with more knowledge and greater expertise than you possess.

In life, you place trust in others based on reputation or a presented persona. Sometimes, that trust is broken; other times, it proves correct. Don't allow broken trust to color your perception of everything and everyone. Especially avoid viewing God through a broken trust lens. He is always trustworthy and faithful. He is at work in ways you cannot see during your time of waiting.

Testing is a Given

Testing is a means of assessment. Even if a doctor is relatively certain about the best treatment for an illness or injury, tests are necessary to confirm. Diagnosis isn't possible without assessing the situation.

This is also true in other areas. If you are dealing with a communication, relationship, financial, spiritual, or any other problem, do the hard work of investigation to determine the underlying causes before you formulate a plan to confront, improve, or eliminate the problem.

During a waiting period in life, you can also reassess areas that need attention. Waiting slows the frantic pace, distancing us from the busyness that often prevents us from addressing issues. View your time of waiting as an opportunity rather than a burden. Take an honest look at patterns, habits, and attitudes that may prevent you from moving forward. Perhaps God is allowing time for you to make changes that will catapult you beyond your waiting room experience.

The time you spend in life's waiting rooms provides the opportunity for self-evaluation. Perhaps you are sidelined to assess your motivations and methods, or to allow you time to refocus, reassess, and seek God's will.

Like all testing, self-assessment can be tedious, stressful, a little frightening, and require patience. While self-examination may shine light on areas you'd rather leave unexposed, what you glean will help you make necessary adjustments and move you forward while you wait.

Practical Matters Need Attention Despite Discomfort

When you arrive at the hospital emergency department, unless unconscious, you still have to go through the intake process. Answering questions, providing insurance information, verifying the accuracy of information already in the system, assessing the injury, relaying symptoms, and determining discomfort level are all part of the process, even if you're in great pain.

In life, even if you're wounded, fearful, distracted, or waiting, practical everyday matters still need your attention. When you are in a holding pattern—a time of waiting—moving forward happens by dealing with the small elements of life that require tending to, even when your mind is occupied with the big issues of your wait. Find a way to continue handling everyday activities, despite fear, frustrations, and distractions.

Sometimes during rote activities, you gain a revelation that provides insight and nudges you forward. These times of revelation may come while doing laundry, walking the dog, waiting in carpool line, or cooking.

Waiting is uncomfortable, something you'd rather have resolved immediately, but by accepting the process, and learning incrementally, you lessen the anxiety and discomfort.

Pain is Part of the Process

Pain is an indicator that something is amiss. Pain also serves as a warning. Without pain, you don't know until it's too late that something is malfunctioning or that injury has occurred.

Pain in life often indicates growth and change. I still remember the "growing pains" of childhood, not only physically, but emotionally. Pay attention to pain. Learn from it. Act on it.

God may allow a time of waiting in your life to slow you long enough to deal with painful experiences you have never processed, to aid healing, and prepare you for what is ahead.

Thankfulness Despite Your Situation

During one ER visit with a loved one, groans, peppered with profanity, came from the next room. From the patient's comments, and those with him, we pieced together his injury. Apparently, a skill saw, coupled with baggy shorts, equaled a snag and drag episode that resulted in a gaping wound up the leg.

While it was easy to think *how dumb*, we all experience times when we set ourselves up for injury. Perhaps you trusted someone again who repeatedly betrayed you, and you were hurt.

Many people incur deep wounds from a variety of sources, none of their choosing. But sometimes, people are so focused on themselves and their troubles they can't see anything positive in their situation. No matter what hard thing you are dealing with, you can always find something for which to be thankful.

No one enjoys waiting, or the uncertainty and anxiety that go along with it, but it is possible to find positives in a season of waiting. The coping skills we develop and insights we discover equip for the future. In time, you may find yourself in a position to help others through a difficult life season.

Some People are Users or Abusers

Emergency department personnel have a label for those who use emergency care instead of going to the doctor's office or to acquire pain medication—"frequent fliers."

Most of us encounter users and abusers occasionally. At first, their neediness and control may trigger mercy and compassion, even love, but eventually we realize their focus is self-centered and we are being used. No matter how much we give, it's never enough to satisfy.

In life's waiting rooms, frequent fliers are those who enjoy one-upping you and your circumstances. Rather than encouraging, they discourage with their tales of woe and negative perspective. Beware the impact they can have on you while you wait and distance yourself.

Next Steps are Your Responsibility

"Treat and Street" is the motto of emergency department personnel. The goal of emergency care is pain relief, assessment, treatment, and release. An emergency is just the first step. What happens after an ER visit—making a followup appointment with a doctor, wound care, filling prescriptions and taking as prescribed—is up to the patient.

It's the same in life. An emergent event that waves a red flag or flashes a blue light needs follow up. Pay attention. Ignoring an issue will not make it disappear. Make sure you take the next steps.

What you do next in a season of waiting is also up to you. If issues exist that prevent you from moving forward now, or when the wait ends, identify what needs work, and do it. Sometimes, we know what needs to change to move forward, but stubbornness prevents us from taking action. Don't prolong a time of waiting because you refuse to take responsibility for changes you need to set in motion.

Focus Your Attention Elsewhere

No matter what you're awaiting—resolution to a situation, the answer to a question, an acceptance or rejection, a birth or death, a medical diagnosis and treatment plan, the next step in a career or relationship—it's easy to become so focused on waiting for that outcome that you can't see anything else. Shift your focus and attention to other areas. Set an exercise goal. Reconnect with those you have put off contacting. Resolution in other areas will provide a sense of accomplishment and lessen the feeling of being in limbo.

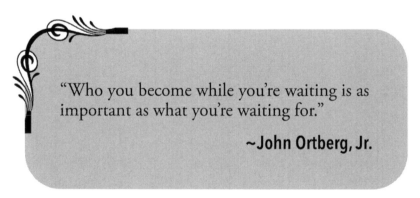

"Who you become while you're waiting is as important as what you're waiting for."

~John Ortberg, Jr.

Learn During the Slow-Down

When our children were young, meanness, disrespect, or disobedience meant a trip to the "thinking stool," also unaffectionately referred to as the "stinking stool." For ten minutes, they had to sit on a certain stool in the den and think about what they had done. For our daughter, being still and waiting for ten minutes to pass was extreme punishment because she was always in motion. The waiting involved in a trip to the "thinking stool" was worse than the contemplation of wrongdoing.

Often, the children begged to get off the stool before the prescribed time frame ended. Occasionally, their sentence was commuted if they could tell me what they learned while thinking about what they had done.

Although it may feel like it, waiting is not punishment. While waiting may push the pause button on one area of life, it doesn't mean you can't move forward in other areas. Consider learning something new or refreshing knowledge or skills you already have. Complete a new project or finish one that was shoved to the back burner a long time ago. Enjoy using your creativity and relish the finished product.

Utilize a waiting period to rest and reflect. Often our lives are so fast paced we rarely allow our bodies and minds time to rejuvenate. Waiting provides much-needed rest, refreshment, and opportunity for reflection.

Watch for Positives

Moving forward while waiting involves growth, spiritual development in the areas of trust, patience, and obedience.

The story of Joseph in the Bible is one of complex emotions. Favoritism, arrogance, jealousy, abuse, forgiveness, and love co-mingle to provide a saga of epic proportions.

Jacob loved his son Joseph more than his other sons. His overt favoritism created jealousy and rivalry. Joseph's brothers plotted to kill him but altered the plan after one brother experienced a bout of conscience. Instead, they sold him to slave traders. Then the brothers lied to their father about what had happened to Joseph, making Jacob believe his son was dead by showing him the multi-colored coat he had given Joseph covered in blood.

Could this story of abuse and deception possibly have a positive outcome? Indeed, it does. God blessed Joseph even though he was in captivity, granting him the favor of his captors, and giving him the ability to interpret dreams.

Pharaoh recognized Joseph's gift as God-given and promoted him from slavery to the position of chief administrator over all of Egypt. Because God revealed to Joseph that years of famine were ahead, he stockpiled grain.

When the famine was at its height, Joseph's brothers appeared before him asking to buy grain. Joseph recognized his brothers, those who had sold him into slavery, but the brothers had no idea the official before them was their brother. It was within Joseph's power to have them arrested, or killed, but he made a different choice.

Joseph was seventeen when his brothers betrayed him, consigning him to a life of slavery. He was thirty when he was elevated to a high government position. The intervening thirteen years were spent in servitude and in prison for an accusation of which he was innocent. Thirteen years is a long time to wait for circumstances to change. What was God doing in Joseph's life during those years? Humbling him? Maturing him? Preparing him?

Joseph could have allowed resentment toward his brothers to fester during those thirteen years. Perhaps anger was an issue he had to work through during this season of waiting. Joseph could have succumbed to discouragement, given up, and rejected God. And once he moved to a position of power, he could have exacted revenge on his brothers when they requested help. Instead, Joseph forgave. His heart was so tender, and his emotions so raw, that at one point he had to leave the room to avoid having his brothers see his tears.

Joseph's waiting years honed him into a man of great wisdom and compassion. God blessed Joseph and positioned him to save his family during years of famine. Although he suffered much because of his brothers' actions and his years of captivity, Joseph recognized and acknowledged God as the source of prosperity and success, saying, "God has caused me to be fruitful and very successful in the land of my suffering" (Genesis 41:52 AMP).

Joseph found the positives in his season of waiting. You can, too.

Fumbling with a False Start

Sometimes, after waiting a long time, everything seems to fall into place to move forward. Roadblocks come down. A detour down a long and circuitous path terminates, placing you back on what appears to be a straight, flat, traffic-less road. You zoom along, confident you are finally making progress and the waiting is over. And then, the road dead-ends.

When athletes "jump the gun" and come off their marks too soon, it's called a false start. Starting before the signal is given to begin is usually unintentional, but happens because a competitor is so revved up anticipation causes him to forge ahead.

When waiting drags on, we sometimes look so intently for a signal the waiting is over we jump ahead when it seems as if all pieces fall into place for us to make a move. Like a keyed-up runner, we dash ahead before a definitive signal comes and rapidly discover roadblocks that send us back to wait at the starting block.

Trusting God and Moving Forward

While it's hard to understand the timing and circumstances surrounding a life pause, waiting is a normal part of life. Sometimes, in our humanness, we blame God for the frustration waiting brings. He already knows your heart, but stating you blame him helps you move forward, tearing down a wall you are unconsciously erecting. Then look for blessings in your current circumstances. Find joy in the small details. Continue to read God's word and ask Him to help you become forward-looking rather than focusing on frustration and impatience.

The apostle Paul encouraged believers to look beyond their current circumstances with expectancy.

> *This resurrection life you received from God is not a timid, grave-tending life. It's adventurously expectant, greeting God with a childlike "What's next, Papa?" God's Spirit touches our spirits and confirms who we really are. We know who he is, and we know who we are: Father and children... We go through exactly what Christ goes through. If we go through the hard times with him, then we're certainly going to go through the good times with him!*

Romans 8:15-17 THE MESSAGE

Reaching Out

Have you waited a long time for physical, mental, or emotional healing? Or have you prayed earnestly for these types of healing for a family member? Luke 8 records a story of a long-awaited healing.

For twelve years, a woman suffered a debilitating health issue. During those years, she had been to doctors, and possibly tried home remedies to go along with what doctors ordered, but no doctor had cured her and nothing she tried changed her situation. Doubtless, she had prayed, asking God for healing, but those petitions went unanswered.

Under Jewish law, this woman would have been considered unclean because her ailment involved continual bleeding. Her designation of "unclean" would have caused people to avoid her, and she was confined to her home, possibly a remote dwelling. Not only was she suffering physically, she was also cut off from the encouragement of others, and perhaps struggling emotionally and mentally because of her isolation.

In her desperation, this woman moved forward. She heard a miracle-worker was nearby, so she left the safety and seclusion of her home and shouldered her way into the pulsing crowd surrounding Jesus. She risked much because at any moment, someone who knew her may have noticed her and yelled "unclean." Yet, she was determined to get close to Jesus, whose reputation as a healer preceded him.

As the crowd jostled, pulling her away and then moving her nearer, she saw the opportunity to reach out and touch the hem of Jesus' clothing. The moment her hand grazed the fabric, the woman was healed. Instantly, she knew healing had occurred. Can you imagine her joy? Her years of waiting were over.

Sometimes, when we are in a prolonged season of waiting, we fail to see that it is possible to move forward even in waiting. For you, moving forward may involve counseling or conversations with trusted friends. Often, instead of reaching out for encouragement and support, we isolate ourselves. Withdrawing in times of difficulty is common, as if we feel we are labeled in the same way this woman in Scripture was designated "unclean."

Moving forward may also mean being honest with yourself about issues and areas in your life that may have precipitated a time of waiting. Did you implement plans without consulting God? Have you allowed others to influence you in ways that do not align with what you know to be God's will? Honest self-assessment is difficult because it reveals what we'd rather not acknowledge, but sometimes it is necessary.

Faithfully waiting for God doesn't mean you can't take some steps forward. And the account in Luke 8 reminds us that a wait that seems interminable can suddenly end.

Jack's Story

After many years as a worship leader, Jack felt God calling him to move his radio ministry to Nashville, TN, but almost immediately, roadblocks appeared that sent Jack and his family into a prolonged season of waiting.

After they listed their house for sale, a downturn in the economy tanked the real estate market. For a year, Jack traveled from South Carolina to Nashville, Tennessee each weekend to produce a national radio show, yet their house never sold. Maybe it's not Nashville, Jack thought.

An interim position became available at a pastor friend's church in Knoxville, TN and Jack began serving there, convinced their home would sell soon. But because their house didn't sell, this position as a worship pastor in Knoxville ended after six months, despite the church wanting him to come on staff full time.

Finally, after two years, the house sold, and Jack and his family wondered where God wanted them to move. Since Jack was still traveling doing itinerant ministry, they moved to another town in South Carolina closer to the airport and made friends. Soon after the move, they believed God wanted them to plant a church. For two-and-a-half years, a group of about forty met in their home, yet despite everything Jack tried, none of those attending their home church were willing to move into any type of leadership roles.

"The people enjoyed coming to our house, and hearing me teach and preach, but I struggled to find some other leaders to step up," said Jack. Taking this as a sign to give up on planting a church, Jack disbanded the group.

A local church that had supported Jack in the church plant effort was suddenly without a pastor. The youth pastor encouraged Jack to submit a resume, but he refused. "I felt God had closed the door, and I wasn't supposed to be a pastor," said Jack.

But one Sunday, he and his wife attended the church to hear the youth pastor preach, who was serving as interim pastor. They fell in love with the people and became involved in a life group. The life group teacher was also the chairman of the pastor search committee. He and Jack became friends, and although he encouraged Jack to submit a resume, he still refused.

After sixteen months, the search committee felt they had found the right person to pastor the church, but when the chairman called, the candidate withdrew his application. Frustrated and confused, the chairman met Jack for a meal and again urged him to consider the pastorate.

During the time the church was without a pastor, Jack preached a few times when the youth pastor was on vacation or had taken the youth group to camp, so the church was familiar with Jack and his preaching. Soon after the other candidate withdrew, the search committee called Jack as pastor at the end of a service, and the members responded with a standing ovation.

It had been seven years since Jack first felt God leading him to pastor a church. Regarding those years of waiting, Jack says, "All I knew to do was keep praying and keep doing what I knew to do until God showed me something different."

Jack and his family continued to live life and move forward while they waited, and that is an example all of us can follow. Don't allow a time of waiting to prevent you from living, learning, and loving while you wait for the next season of life.

Taking Next Steps While Waiting

Moving forward without a clear path and a definite destination takes courage and faith. If you are a detail-oriented person, not knowing the exact destination challenges your ability to make a move. Taking the next logical step, while not running ahead of God, requires the ability to quell your own desires and impatience, while listening closely for God's voice.

Those the Bible refers to as "heroes of the faith" were ordinary people who displayed extraordinary faith, trusting God to take them on journeys with uncertain routes and destinations. All of those mentioned in Hebrews 11 (Abel, Enoch, Noah, Abraham, Sarah, Isaac, Jacob, Joseph, Moses, Rahab, Gideon, Barak, Samson, Jephthah, David, and Samuel) had to trust God and take steps forward while waiting for additional revelation and future directions.

Like Jack and his family, they took the next logical step, by faith.

King David's 30-Year Wait

The time from Samuel's anointing of David the shepherd boy until David the king took the throne spanned a period of almost thirty years. During those years, David served King Saul as a warrior and musician, and eventually became his son-in-law. But those waiting years were turbulent, and much of the time, David was under attack, on the run, or in hiding from enemy nations and his father-in-law, whose jealousy prompted him to attempt to murder David several times.

Thirty years is a long time to wait, but even though David knew he would one day be king, he continued to view Saul as God's appointed ruler. The psalms provide a record of some of David's fears and frustrations during his years of waiting, but they also document his trust and reliance on God.

Whether your season of waiting is years, months, weeks, or days, look for God's direction and protection. If God has revealed something ahead for you, trust it will come to pass in his timing. Allow hope to bolster you when discouragement overwhelms, and trust God for each step of your journey.

Let all that I am wait quietly before God, for my hope is in him.

Psalm 62:5 NLT

Encourage the Watchers and Waiters

People watch to see how we handle life's difficulties. Sometimes, this kind of observation feels oppressive, but it can also spur us to learn from what we are experiencing and use those insights to encourage others.

Sometimes we are reluctant to let others know we are struggling. We like to portray an image that conveys we are calm and in control, so we don't talk about hardships. But Scripture prompts us to "encourage one another and build each other up" (1 Thessalonians 5:11 NLT).

Perhaps you feel you can't encourage others because you are still in waiting mode, or you have nothing positive to convey. Even if you are experiencing extreme frustration, you are learning and growing. Spend some time examining what God is revealing to you and pray for opportunities to encourage others.

Encouragement Changes Perspectives

Perhaps you are more of a critiquer than an encourager, seeing first what could be tweaked to make situations or people better. If so, shifting to encourager mode takes some effort. But one outcome of becoming an encourager is it trains you to see positives before you see negatives. Being an encourager changes your perspective. The process may take a while, but looking for positives and speaking words of encouragement rewires your criticism circuits.

Encouragement Builds Up

Many people are beaten down by their past, or their current circumstances, or both. For some, their upbringing was a nightmarish confusion of abuse, criticism, and discouragement. When you grow up in that type of environment, it warps your perspective of people and the world. It takes real effort to move forward, gain self-worth, recognize positives, and be an encourager to others.

Conversely, if you grew up with love and encouragement, realize you are blessed, and make it your goal to pass along that love and encouragement to others. Being an encourager can be as simple as saying "How are you today?" to someone you see every day, but don't really know. Your genuine expression of interest may be the only hint of caring the person receives that day.

Another facet of being an encourager is cultivating the art of listening. Encouraging isn't just pep-talking; it's listening and hearing the fears, frustrations, and needs between the speaker's words. What are the real issues and how can you speak wisdom? Look for opportunities to compliment, listen, encourage, and support those you encounter.

Encouragement Takes Your Mind Off Self

When you are waiting, or dealing with other types of challenges, it's easy to become self-focused. Perhaps you feel sorry for yourself because you are in one of life's valleys and no one is stepping up to encourage you. Instead, look around you. Others are in similar hard seasons, struggling with difficulties just as you are. Looking beyond your own discouragement, while speaking words of encouragement to another, shifts your focus. Never underestimate the impact reaching out to another person in a manner you wish someone would respond to you has on your life.

Encouragement Sets a Positive Example

The current climate in our world is one of fault-finding, criticism, negativism, and slander, and those voices are loud and strong. In building others up, you set a positive example in a culture that seeks to tear others down. It takes intentionality to resist that mindset and be a positive voice, but each person who chooses encouragement over criticism promotes a different perspective. Decide to be a voice of encouragement to someone today.

Chapter 11

Experiencing Peace in Waiting

You will keep in perfect and constant peace the one
whose mind is steadfast [that is, committed and
focused on You—in both inclination and character],
Because he trusts and takes refuge in You [with hope
and confident expectation].

Isaiah 26:3 AMP

Trust, hope, and confident expectation are easy to state, but much more difficult to implement. Finding peace while you wait is challenging. Impatience knocks at the door, tempting you to forge ahead; to make something happen. But pushing forward when the message is pause, may make your situation worse than your time of waiting.

Deterrents to Peace

We all experience times in life when personal peace is hard to find. Invisible enemies rob us of peace and create an environment of unrest.

Assumptions

Assuming you understand a situation, or the intent, thoughts, or motivation of a person is arrogant and unrealistic. Assigning thoughts and feelings to others imposes your perspective when you really have no concept of what others think or feel without asking.

In recent months, I have seen or heard long diatribes from those claiming to "educate" on various topics. With those rants come the assumption that I am not intelligent enough to do my research and think for myself. Assumptions diminish the capabilities of others and prompt words or actions without allowing another perspective.

Expectations

Unmet expectations are one of the greatest causes of conflict and conflict negates peace. Thinking others will respond based on your expectations of them is a sure path to disappointment and misunderstanding. Only through open communication can expectations be conveyed, discussed, altered, or met.

Often, we have unrealistic expectations of others and ourselves. Those who expect a lot of themselves usually transfer those expectations to others, creating frustration when people don't respond as they assume. Lowering expectations and extending grace creates an atmosphere of peace.

Anger

Increasingly, examples of unbridled anger emerge in our world. This anger doesn't necessarily stem from outrage over injustice. Often, anger plays out over something small like someone not realizing a long line forms behind where he entered it. Instead of calmly explaining to the perceived line-jumper that the line begins in a different location, those around him berate with profanity.

Sometimes, people are angry without really knowing the root cause. Perhaps a comment touches a feeling of inadequacy or ignites a flame of long-ago bullying or abuse. Despite the reasons for anger, failing to tame anger ensures a life devoid of peace.

Negativism

Now, more than ever, we live in a world where negativism rules, creating an environment of divisiveness and tension. Media outlets bombard daily with discouraging reports, while positive news goes unreported. Conditions are not ideal, but despite struggles, we remain a blessed people.

While identifying positives amid negatives may be challenging, start by looking at elements in day-to-day life that are gifts: evening birdsong, a gentle rain, colorful flowers, the interaction of family preparing and sharing a meal, the brilliant hues of a sunrise or sunset.

Not everything in life is negative and strident. Look for, and savor, moments of tranquility and peace. Provide an environment of peace in your home by approaching difficult discussions without raised voices, and by limiting negative or violent programing.

Guilt

I heard a woman say she has always experienced a pervading since of guilt. Any time an authority figure asks to see her, she immediately assumes she has done something wrong. When the opposite is true, and she is thanked or praised for her work, she is surprised.

Unrelenting guilt, and its tag-along regret, can rob you of peace in a way unequaled to other peace-robbing culprits. Freeing yourself of guilt is a multi-step process that involves admission and forgiveness.

If there is something you can fix with admission and apology, do it. If guilt stems from an ancient injustice, confess it to God, accept his forgiveness, then forgive yourself.

Another cause of guilt may stem from someone who conditioned you to take the blame for everything—even when you weren't at fault. This source of guilt is more difficult to purge and may require counseling. Take steps to deal with guilt and don't allow it to ride roughshod over your life again. Freedom from guilt leads to peace.

Finding Personal Peace in Turbulent Times

We live in uncertain times. Our world is rife with unrest, dissatisfaction, and fear. When this turbulent climate is coupled with upheaval on a personal level—in the form of relationship issues, emotional turmoil, financial stress, or a time of waiting—it feels as if life is a whirl of problems and urgent issues that vie for our time and attention.

Experiencing peace is challenging when this level of commotion is unrelenting, even for those who remain calm in most situations. So, let's examine some methods of finding peace in turbulent times.

Seek Wisdom

Many people view Scripture as antiquated and out of touch with reality. However, Scripture overflows with wisdom relevant for today. Current culture is not the first filled with uncertainty, injustice, abuse, political unrest, wars, and rumors of war. Much of Scripture deals with people living in captivity or under the laws of authoritarian conquest. Fear, injustice, and persecution were prevalent, as they are today. People often waited years for the fulfillment of promises, or an end to suffering.

Study this wisdom and apply it to your life. "Wisdom and knowledge will be the stability of your times" (Isaiah 33:6 NKJV).

Shut Out Loud, Strident Voices

Social media is filled with loud voices that negate personal peace. Of course, the solution for this is to refrain from social media, but often we are so engaged we return again and again to this source of turmoil. And when we're not on social media, we're mentally formulating a response, even if we never post our thoughts. While there are benefits to connecting with others, the negatives of social media interaction often outweigh the positives.

Sometimes, strident voices are closer to home as a friend or family member feels compelled to voice opinions, provide unwanted advice, or draw you into debate. Resist, if possible. However, if you can't escape the person, memorize the words to a song or a passage of scripture you can silently recall during the diatribe. This is one scenario when it is acceptable to not pay attention!

See Beyond Current Circumstances

One of the biggest challenges of finding peace is cultivating the ability to realize what is currently happening is not a permanent situation. The circumstances you are experiencing right now, a waiting period of indeterminate length, perhaps with some other type of stress-producing situation, aren't necessarily indicative of what you can expect from now on. Just as the sun reappears after a deluge of rain, so turbulent times moderate, seasons of waiting end, and tranquility ensues.

Employ Mustard-Seed Faith

When I was young, I had a charm bracelet. It was a treat to look at charms in a store and receive permission to purchase one. A favorite charm was a tiny canister of mustard seeds with Matthew 17:20 visible beside the seeds. "If your faith is the size of a mustard seed, you can say to this mountain, 'Move from here to there,' and it will move" (GW).

As a pre-teen, those tiny seeds intrigued me, and when coupled with words about faith, made an impression on me. The concept of something so small being powerful enough to move something so big underscored that what is possible in the spiritual realm is far different from the natural world.

Mustard-seed faith hops barriers and navigates around obstacles. Mustard-seed faith is persistent in prayer, yet waits for answers. Mustard-seed faith results in peace.

Give Up Worry

I've heard people say, "I give my concerns to God and then I snatch them right back." This statement indicates they have a difficult time relinquishing control and don't trust God with the outcome of their concerns. Trusting God requires practice, but the more you do it, the easier it becomes.

Ultimately, even if your worst fears are realized, God promises to make any difficult journey with you, in the waiting and beyond. A relationship with God is the key to personal peace. No matter what circumstances you encounter in your life, or how turbulent world events, God will never leave you. In seasons of waiting, relinquish your worries and fears to God, believing he is aware of your situation and capable of handling all you give him.

The Steadfast Mind

The definition of "steadfast" is firmly fixed in one place, not subject to change, immovable, firm in belief, determination, or adherence. Remaining steadfast while in life's waiting rooms is hard. Fears, discouragement, anger, and uncertainty chip away at your resolve to remain steadfast. Then, suddenly, you're not as sure of God's promises and a little less firm in your belief that this time of waiting will end with a positive result.

Steadfastness begins with the mind and moves to the heart. Taking every thought captive and assessing each are crucial to maintaining a positive outlook and peace in times of waiting. Taking thoughts captive involves not allowing your mind to run rampant with potential scenarios of how your time of waiting is going to play out. Often, when we are in a stressful situation, our thoughts follow a negative path rather than a positive one. When your mind heads in a negative direction, stop and pray. Ask God to help you redirect your thoughts and voice your trust in God's provision.

A steadfast mind is strengthened by focusing on verses about God's timing, faithfulness, promises, provision, and peace. Then experience peace as you trust God for what happens next. The only way to experience peace as you wait is to relinquish control, accept God's timing, and trust him for what happens next.

The Prolonged Wait

When waiting drags on, remaining at peace with your situation is challenging. Like the ebb and flow of tides, peace comes and goes. The unresolved element of waiting creates feelings of helplessness. Trust waivers and discouragement threatens to overwhelm. Consider the following questions to help process and overcome discouragement.

What is the Root of Your Discouragement?

On the surface, this question seems like a no-brainer. Obviously, waiting is the source of discouragement, but is it?

As a writer, I have experienced discouragement when I see others advancing in their writing journey when mine seems to be stagnant. Perhaps you are dealing with something similar and feeling left behind while others move forward. Comparisons fuel discouragement. Your journey is not like anyone else's so don't use the progress of others as a barometer.

When I returned to writing after a season of caregiving followed by a season of grief, I felt as if I could never regain the traction I once had in the writing community. In some ways I didn't, but new avenues opened, and I could move forward.

Are You Trying to Impose Your Time Frame?

Most of us segment our lives in terms of goals and events. Waiting pushes pause on some of our goals and places some events in suspended animation. It's almost impossible to speculate about when pause will shift to forward and suspended animation return to motion. As hard as it is, try to accept the fluid time frame of waiting. Capture positives and elements of peace in each day without imposing a wishful time frame on tomorrow. "Refuse to worry about tomorrow, but deal with each challenge that comes your way, one day at a time. Tomorrow will take care of itself" (Matthew 6:34 TPT).

Is Your Trust Shaky?

Many people struggle with trust, especially if a promised experience or reward failed to materialize. During life pauses, it's common to place trust in connections or projections, to trust doing rather than resting and waiting. In our hearts, we know God is trustworthy, but in our heads, we think we should take action. Trust requires relinquishing your own efforts to God. This is not always a one-and-done activity. Effectively trusting may mean giving discouragement, fears, frustrations, and control to God daily, or multiple times a day. Don't berate yourself for having to bolster your trust repeatedly. That doesn't mean you are faithless.

Is Your Peace Contingent on the Ultimate Outcome?

Courage is an essential element of peace. Sometimes we think of courage only in terms of bravery and the fortitude required to face and battle against an opponent. But courage is also the strength to persevere and withstand difficulty.

In times of waiting, peace comes not in knowing when the wait will end and what the outcome of waiting will be, but in having the courage to trust and persevere through the ups and downs of the journey.

Are You Holding on to Hope?

After nine years of marriage, my parents remained without children. My father came from a family of eleven and my mother from a family of seven, so childless was a hard place to be. I'd like to say they were still holding on to hope, but I'm not sure that was the case.

Later that year, my mother went to the doctor because she feared she had cancer. She was shocked to learn her malady was something else entirely, a nine-month condition that culminated with my birth. While my parents' prayers were answered, and hope restored, you may long for something that never comes to fruition. Perhaps you hope to love and be loved, wish for a job opportunity that never quite materializes, pray for a family member to finally address a devastating addiction, or long for a cure for a chronic illness.

Hope is crucial in waiting because it keeps you looking forward instead of giving up. Hope allows you to find fulfillment and experience peace even when life doesn't turn out as you planned.

Marva's Story

"Many little girls fantasize about their Boaz, the Prince Charming husband they plan to marry in their 20s or 30s. Like Ruth's Boaz in the Bible, this ideal husband would love, provide, and protect her and their children.

"I was such a girl. I had it all planned. I would marry in my late 20s, have two children, and live happily in a brick house with a gazebo in the backyard. But my 20s passed, followed by anxious 30s, 40s, 50s, and now, in my later 60s, still no Boaz.

"In Psalm 37:4, David said, 'Delight yourself in the Lord and he will give you the desires of your heart.' I love you Lord. I thought I delighted in you, so what happened? Where is my Boaz? What happened to our two children and the gazebo?

God Gives Unexpected Answers

"Through bits of revelation, the Holy Spirit gradually answered my questions. First, I realized the Lord gave me children, but not the way I had imagined. Along with nurturing children while teaching school, he also gave me a very special assignment. I had the opportunity to "mother" three adults—two much older than I and one five years younger.

"Each of my unexpected children had unique personalities. One was strong-willed and one was sweet and even-tempered. The third had special needs. While I was looking for Boaz, my aunt, father, and brother needed extra care. Their mothers were no longer alive, but I was. If I had been married, I would not have been able to spend the extra time and energy needed for their care. My husband would have either been neglected, or I would have had to choose between him and them.

God Guides Us to Wait

"Over the years, a few men asked for my hand in marriage, but the Holy Spirit gave me wisdom, revealing major spiritual, cultural, emotional, or age differences which could easily have torn a marriage apart. If I had married any of these men, the marriage probably would not have lasted. The men were not terrible, we just did not fit each other.

God Waits for my Obedience

"What God reveals can be hurtful, even when it is in my best interest. The Holy Spirit had me inspect myself, then asked if I were the person Boaz would want to marry. Unfortunately, the answer was no. I had back problems, needed hip replacement surgery, was obese, had emotional baggage, and I was so busy being an over-protective "mother" I hardly had time to breathe. Really, who would want to marry someone with all those issues? Thankfully, most have been resolved, although my weight is still a work in progress.

"The man I have for you also has areas of needed improvement, came the Holy Spirit's inner voice. I am waiting for both of you to become obedient, get your acts together, and do those things I have already put in your hearts.

"Boaz and I are probably each 60+ years old. One would think we would have our acts together by now. Apparently not.

Wisdom Gained While Waiting

"Life's best experiences are never of our orchestration. The Lord brought all things together for my good long before I ever knew anything about them. Romans 8:28 reminds us, 'And we know that all things work together for good to those who love God, to those who are called according to His purpose.'

"I remember wonderful experiences God allowed in my life that were entirely different, yet better than what I imagined.

"During my last month or two of high school, a new program, Student Support Services, chose me and several other students for a scholarship, loan, work-study college opportunity. My mother's plan for my college financing had fallen through in January of that year.

"Decades later, after retirement, the Lord gave me an appointment for a job interview I had not applied for and I got the job!

I was ready to sign a contract for a condo, which had a few features I needed, but the owner of another condo, which was not for sale yet, knocked on my door looking for a realtor to sell her home. My realtor worked with both of us, and I got the condo that fit all my needs. It even has an electric fireplace which I had thought about only once.

"Each of these examples are parts of long stories which include ways I tried to solve the problems on my own but failed. God has always answered my prayers at unexpected times, so why would I think Boaz would come when I expected?

"Through the years, God has continued to give me direction. God has been, and still is, my comforter, friend, provider, and more. He is so trustworthy. We have a wonderful relationship. He loves me, and I strive to show my love toward Him.

"I now know, the Lord answers prayers in his way, at the right time, for my good, when everything is ready. This wisdom, obtained while waiting for Boaz, has taught me to trust and patiently wait for the Lord's answers and guidance in every situation. So, I will continue to have faith, trusting the Lord wholeheartedly rather than relying on my understanding."

Chapter 12

Recognizing the Rewards of Waiting

The Lord is good to those who wait for him, to the soul who seeks him.

Lamentations 3:25 ESV

My father was a builder, and over the course of his career, constructed many rental properties. The economy was prospering, and rental property was a money-making proposition. After his death, the income from those properties helped to support my mother, but as the economy shifted and the properties aged, upkeep ate into proceeds.

After my mother's death, I inherited the rental properties. By this point, some were in declining neighborhoods and showed evidence of deferred maintenance. In my limited vision, I viewed ownership as a burden because maintaining the properties and keeping them rented drained financially and added stress to my already hectic life. Years later, when the market improved, I sold the properties. Only then did I view them as assets.

Life pauses are similar. When you are sidelined in a waiting period, it feels like a burden because your goals and plans are deferred. You imagine yourself missing opportunities as those around you move forward with their lives. You are stuck in an uncomfortable situation, over which you have no control, and all thoughts track toward the time when waiting is over.

You may experience anxiety similar to the anxiousness I felt at suddenly owning and shouldering responsibility for rental properties. Only after you have completed the journey, can you look back and see how waiting was beneficial. The positive aspects of waiting often surface well beyond the end of a season of waiting.

With inherited rental property, I could have panicked, placed all for sale in a sluggish market, and gotten far less for them than they were worth. Instead, I waited, which wasn't easy given ongoing repairs, difficult tenants, increasing property taxes, and 4:00 AM maintenance emergencies. But ultimately, waiting was to my advantage. By waiting, I redeemed the full value of my inheritance.

Waiting Examples and Rewards in Scripture

> *Therefore, the Lord will wait, that He may be gracious to you; And therefore He will be exalted, that He may have mercy on you. For the Lord is a God of justice; Blessed are all those who wait for Him.*

Isaiah 30:18 NKJV

Scripture reminds us God is gracious, merciful, and patient with his wayward, disobedient children. Even in disappointment and anger, God waits, providing additional time for us to return to him when we stray.

We are not always as patient and merciful to those in our lives. Sometimes, we give up on people and relationships that we view as frustrating, time-consuming, and not worth our effort. But God modeled waiting, and Scripture provides numerous accounts of those who experienced seasons of waiting and were rewarded for their obedience and patience.

Forty Days in the Wilderness

The usual way to view Jesus' forty days in the wilderness is as a time of testing and overcoming temptation, but have you ever considered his sojourn in the wilderness as a time of waiting? A season of waiting doesn't have to be long to qualify. Waiting may be brief, perhaps only a matter of hours or days, but this compressed time frame doesn't change the emotions or frustrations.

For those who have experienced long periods of waiting, forty days doesn't sound like much, but have you gone without food for that long or been without the encouragement of others when you faced a monumental hurdle? The challenges we encounter in times of waiting are unique to each of us. What others do not struggle with in waiting may be a big obstacle for you.

Likewise, what God teaches you through waiting may differ from what he teaches others. The timing of waiting also varies, crafted in a manner that allows for growth and the positioning of circumstances and events so they align for our benefit.

Jesus' sojourn in the wilderness happened immediately after a spiritual high, following his baptism. Jesus heard words of praise and affirmation from his father, but then Scripture says the Spirit whisked Jesus to the wilderness. As with our times of waiting, Jesus had no control over the timing. Unlike times when he withdrew to a solitary place for prayer, Jesus did not choose this desert experience. These days of waiting and testing were part of God's plan.

The wilderness location is interesting. In the desert, there was no one to help or give counsel other than God. If we realize early in our waiting that God is our best resource, our time in the desert of waiting is much easier to endure. However, emotions often cloud that realization.

One of the most significant lessons we derive from Jesus' forty days of waiting is how he successfully battled Satan. Jesus relied on scriptural truths to sustain and power him through the struggles of waiting. We can do the same. Jesus spoke Scripture. There is power in the spoken word, but you can also gain insight and strength from writing Scripture, meditating on it, and memorizing it.

Memorization of Scripture provides a ready arsenal to combat Satan's lies. Using the wisdom and power found in Scripture— and applying it to life situations—provides encouragement and support.

Jesus' forty days of waiting were preparation for the challenges he would face in his ministry. His time on earth was all about waiting until the appointed time to fulfill his mission, and this desert experience was part of the process.

Building a Temple

King David wanted to build a temple for the Lord. The inequity of his opulent palace juxtaposed against the tent that housed the Ark of the Covenant bothered David. His desire to build a temple for the Lord was not a goal to bring glory to himself, but to honor God.

Despite his good intentions, God spoke through the prophet Nathan, telling David he was not the man for the job. David's many years as a warrior disqualified him. Instead, God assigned the building of the temple to David's son Solomon, a man of wisdom and peace.

David reacted in a way many of us might not when given a roadblock of this magnitude. Instead of arguing with God, or going ahead with the project anyway, David praised God, acknowledging God's blessing on him and his household.

The depth of David's relationship with God is evident in his response. Although God forbade David from involvement in the actual construction, he gathered funds and materials and prepared plans for the temple's construction. Later, Solomon assembled workers and oversaw the seven-year construction of the temple.

Several insights are clear from this account. First, David obeyed God without question when God said wait. He did not complain, argue, pout, or sidestep God when he put a full stop on David's plan. Second, our plans are not always in line with God's. Even when we think we have a great idea, it's not always within God's will or time frame. And third, David accepted God's directive with thanksgiving and praise.

David serves as a role model for us regarding seasons of waiting. By his example, we learn how to respond when God says wait.

Building a Boat

If Noah had lived in today's world, he'd be branded as a lunatic. Actually, even in his day, people thought Noah was a few sheep short of a herd for building a boat in his backyard when there was no water around. This boat was no canoe. It was the size of one and a half football fields or roughly half the size of the ill-fated Titanic. God gave Noah specific instructions about how to build the ark and what animals and people to load onto it. Noah obeyed.

Waiting was involved in building the ark, in the rain and flooding, and then in the waiting period before anyone could leave the ark. Noah was 500 years old when God told him to build an ark. He was 600 when the floodgates of heaven opened and the springs within the earth overflowed. One hundred years is a long time to wait for the completion of a project, yet Noah did not give up during his season of waiting. The flood lasted one hundred and fifty days, and the water receded for one hundred and fifty days, and the land dried for approximately sixty-five days.

A year in a boat, with a zoo, is a long season of waiting, yet Noah did not rush ahead of God's timing. As soon as his feet hit land, he built an altar and worshiped God. Noah's obedience, persistence in following God's directives, and patience saved his life and the lives of his family members, and ensured the continuation of mankind.

The Rewards of Obedience

As I watch our children teach our grandchildren to obey, I'm reminded that even little children have a willful sin nature that causes them to reject authority and push established boundaries. Delaying, pretending not to hear, bargaining, and begging for one more chance before punishment are classic strategies of the disobedient child.

As adults, we aren't much different in how we approach God. We delay when he prompts, pretend not to hear when confronted with areas of sin, bargain to change what's involved in obedience, and beg for another chance when consequences come. Despite the abundant rewards of obedience, all of us are resistant to obeying God.

Each of us makes hundreds of choices daily. They may be inconsequential, or life-altering. The book of Deuteronomy clearly outlines the benefits of wise choices, and the consequences of poor ones. Deuteronomy 28 promises that with obedience comes fertility, victory over enemies, esteem, possessions, and abundant prosperity. Verse 13 promises if we follow God's commands we'll always come out on top, even if waiting is involved at some point.

In contrast, disobedience results in living under God's curse. Disobedience promises a life of defeat, suffering, disease, and destruction. This sounds extremely harsh, but God wanted to get the attention of his people then and now.

With the pros and cons clearly lined out, it's hard to imagine any of us choosing disobedience, but we often do. However, as is typical of God's mercy, he provides us with recourse for bad decisions. As a loving parent, God doesn't abandon us, kill us, or forget his covenant with us when we mess up.

Scripture promises that when we're in distress, we have the option to return to the Lord and obey him. It's comforting to know repentance is the only thing standing between our mistakes and a restored relationship with God.

Benefits of Waiting

During a period of economic downturn, I watched an online presentation about how people respond to a volatile market. The presenter used a visual to help make his point. He held out one hand, and with a hammer in the other hand, pretended to pound his outstretched hand.

The presenter explained when we experience something uncomfortable or painful, we make decisions based on an overwhelming desire to get away. He said investors often make rash decisions to move or sell their assets when markets plummet because they feel such intense anxiety about their losses. What they fail to realize is waiting ultimately brings greater profit.

In times of waiting, trusting that rewards lie ahead is difficult because everything about the situation feels uncomfortable, uncontrollable, and unwieldy. However, with focused attention you can find positives in your present situation, and condition yourself to hold back and wait, rather than dashing forward with decisions that may prove disastrous.

The 3 R's

COVID pushed the pause button on the way we normally conduct our lives. We went from being able to go where we wanted, when we wanted, to staying in our homes with only occasional trips out for necessary provisions. Streets that were once crowded with traffic were suddenly empty as people waited for the unknown.

Many were uncomfortable with the slowdown and ill-at-ease with the new normal as they waited for the situation to change. But waiting provides opportunity for rest, reflection, and renewal, and allows us to refocus for even greater perspective.

Rest

For twenty-five years, I participated in a 5:30 a.m. cycling class three mornings a week. While I enjoyed the camaraderie of fellow cyclists and benefited from the exercise this challenging class provided, I often didn't do a good job of going to bed early enough to get proper rest.

When the fitness center suddenly closed its doors, and the cycling class disbanded, I felt displaced. But the change to my schedule resulted in added rest that enhanced my mental capabilities and energy level throughout the day. I didn't stop exercising altogether, just changed to a later time.

Although many people view a time of waiting negatively, one benefit is the opportunity to slow down from life's frantic pace and rest. Yet, we often find it difficult to let go of our plans and schedules and take advantage of rest. Sometimes we equate rest with laziness. Instead, view rest as an opportunity for physical recuperation, mental stimulation, and emotional rejuvenation.

Reflection

Many of us avoid quietness and stillness. We're a blur of constant motion, moving from one activity to the next, listening to music or TV, checking social media, reading online articles, or playing games on our phones. While moving, talking, or engaging in mindless pursuits, there is no time to reflect, ponder, process emotions, or connect spiritually.

Waiting allows time for contemplation and reflection and an opportunity to process thoughts and feelings and hear God's voice. For those unaccustomed to stillness, it may take time to adjust to the cessation of motion reflection requires. But once you begin to experience the peace and personal revelations, you will look forward to times of reflection with anticipation.

Renewal

After my mother's death, my family home needed renovation and renewal. My father died almost twenty years before my mother, and he always took care of maintenance and repairs. Without him there, maintenance in many areas of the house was left undone. Some rooms needed a total gut job, others, a good cleaning and a coat of paint. The job was projected to last three months. In reality, it required much longer. When the renovation was complete, I could feel my daddy's approval even though he wasn't present.

Renewal in times of waiting is similar. It may appear to require minimal effort, but once you begin, you discover there is more work required than you realized. You may need to take some habits, actions, reactions, and attitudes down to the studs and start over.

Spiritual renewal may mean in-depth study of God's word. Physical renewal could start with cultivating an exercise routine and sticking with it or shifting to a plan of healthier eating. Each step you take toward renewal refreshes, helps you cope with your current circumstances, prepares you for the next turn in your journey, and more closely aligns you to the Father's plans and purposes for your life.

Honor not Servitude

Periods of waiting in our lives often feel like indentured servitude, but, with perception, you will discover rewards.

For centuries, queens, princesses, and other nobility have had ladies-in-waiting. While this title sounds like a position of servitude, instead, it is one of honor. Ladies-in-waiting are noblewomen, who serve as personal assistants to royalty in a variety of ways.

The Queen of England, Queen Elizabeth, has nine ladies-in-waiting, some needed daily and others only for ceremonial occasions. Although unpaid, ladies-in-waiting enjoy other forms of compensation, including flexible schedules, travel expenses, a wardrobe allowance, job security, prestige, and a close relationship with those they serve.

Any time you are chosen for a position, the initial excitement gives way to the reality of the duties and obligations the position entails. Honor always comes with responsibility. Like ladies-in-waiting, effort goes with the title.

In waiting, look for what God is teaching you. Accept that while you feel as if you're in limbo, it is an honor to serve a God who cares about you so much he would place you in a waiting period for your growth, protection, or to position events to inure to your benefit.

Readiness

Be ready for action, and have your lamps burning.
Be like servants waiting to open the door at
their master's knock when he returns from a
wedding. Blessed are those servants whom the master
finds awake when he comes. I can guarantee this
truth: He will change his clothes, make them sit
down at the table, and serve them.

Luke 12:35-37 GW

While this passage of Scripture refers to Jesus' return, it also speaks to readiness and rewards. Waiting can lull us into stagnation, cause us to stop looking forward, and assume the end of waiting is not imminent, especially when the time drags on. But readiness in waiting is linked to rewards. In the scenario in this passage, the reward for readiness suggests the servants become the honored guests. Remaining hopefully expectant in waiting prepares you to move forward and receive rewards when the wait is over.

A Promised Gift

[Jesus] appeared to his apostles and spoke to them
about God's kingdom. While he was still with
them, he said: "Don't leave Jerusalem yet. Wait
here for the Father to give you the Holy Spirit, just
as I told you he has promised to do."

Acts 1:3-4 CEV

Who doesn't enjoy receiving a gift? When our grandchildren see gift bags at a family gathering, the first question is "who are those presents for?" Even if they learn the gift isn't theirs, they remain in anticipatory mode, standing at the ready to help with the unwrapping, admire the contents, and enjoy the festivities.

Jesus appeared to his disciples and spoke of events yet to come, he gave them specific instructions: don't leave, wait here. If they had failed to follow his directives, they would have missed out on a wonderful, promised gift, the gift of the Holy Spirit.

Some of us struggle with following instructions. Either we think we know a better way, or we're too impatient to take the time to read an instruction manual. We attempt assembly or installation based on our knowledge. Often those attempts end badly.

What is really behind failure to heed instructions? Self-sufficiency? Impatience? Feeling you know more than the instructor?

Suppose Jesus' disciples hadn't followed his directive to stay and wait. What if impatience and eagerness for the next season of life had propelled them to leave Jerusalem and strike out on missionary journeys without waiting for the promised gift? They would have denied themselves the power, perception, and comfort of the Holy Spirit, and attempted a task far beyond their personal capabilities.

Jesus referred to the Holy Spirit as the Comforter. When we are instructed to wait, the comfort, peace, and wisdom the Holy Spirit provides are our greatest rewards for paying attention to the directive to stay where we are and wait instead of rushing ahead.

In all seasons of life, the Holy Spirit provides divine instruction, perception, peace, and comfort. If we are tuned in and receptive, we benefit.

Waiting and Seeking

The Lord is wonderfully good to those who wait for him, to those who seek for him.

Lamentations 3:25 TLB

Waiting is hard. Like a boxcar on a forgotten sidetrack, waiting forces us to remain in place and watch as the express trains speed by. But Lamentations reminds us that waiting for God and seeking God, make us the beneficiaries of His wonderful goodness.

In your time of waiting, are you also seeking the Lord? To seek means to go in search of; to ask for; to make an attempt. Seeking requires action. You have to pursue the wonderful good God has for you in times of waiting. Don't allow anger, frustration, pride, or haste to rob you of the gift of waiting. That's right, waiting is a gift. Embrace it. Utilize it. Learn from it. And as you wait, draw closer to God.

The next season is on the horizon. Trust God to move you forward, in his timing, to all that awaits.

ENDNOTES

Portions of *Life on Pause* are excerpted from the following posts on Candy's blog, *Forward Motion.* www.CandyArrington.com/blog

"When Life Hands You Roadblocks and Detours" 6-6-18

"Finding Perspective" 3-21-18

"Establishing Roots" 7-10-19

"Remembrance, Sacrifice, and Freedom" 5-25-20

"3 Reasons to Encourage Others" 3-13-19

"Lessons from a Night in the ER" 7-18-18

"Finding Personal Peace in Turbulent Times" 5-30-18

"7 Enemies of Peace" 6-10-20

Additional excepts from previously published devotionals:

"In Everything, Give Thanks" - CBN.com ©2011 Candy Arrington

"You are Excused" – Arisedaily.com – March 2, 2019

About the Author

Candy Arrington is a writer, blogger, and speaker. She frequently writes on the topics of faith, health, personal growth, and methods for moving through, and beyond, challenging life circumstances. Candy's publishing credits include other nonfiction books and hundreds of articles and stories in numerous print and online outlets including *Focus on the Family, AriseDaily.com, Inspiration.org, CBN.com, Healthgrades.com, Care.com, NextAvenue.org, CountryLiving.com,* and *Writer's Digest.*

Candy gains writing inspiration from vintage photographs, historic architecture, nature, and the application of Scripture to everyday life. She enjoys teaching at writing conferences, guiding writers in how to best craft their ideas to experience publishing success.

Candy and her husband, Jim, live in upstate South Carolina and love their roles as Glam-Glam and Bop to their three precious grandchildren.

To learn more, visit CandyArrington.com where you can read and sign up to receive her blog, *Forward Motion.*

Bible Versions

Made in the USA
Columbia, SC
09 May 2021